The Secret Sayings of The Living Jesus

The Secret Sayings
of The Living Jesus

Studies in the Coptic
Gospel According to Thomas
by Ray Summers

WORD BOOKS

WACO, TEXAS

Contents

Acknowledgements

The author extends grateful acknowledgement

To

Southwestern Baptist Theological Seminary

Whose administration and faculty extended the invitation for a lectureship which made necessary the completion of this work

Whose faculty and student body listened with varying degrees of patience and interest to the delivery of the lectures February 1967

To

Mrs. Paul C. Higginbotham

Whose endowment of the *Day-Higginbotham* Lectures as a memorial to her husband and parents, Mr. and Mrs. Riley Day, made possible the delivery of these as the initial series in that lectureship

To

Kendrick Grobel

Whose scholarly commitment first interested and instructed me in Coptic

Whose exchange through conference and correspondence of ideas on *The Gospel According to Thomas* helped this material to grow toward production

Whose warm and delightful friendship lingers to bless beyond his untimely passing

Introduction

"The Judeo-Christian Faith," "The Ecumenical Church," "Christianity"—words! They speak of a tremendous movement in the religions of mankind—man's search for an understanding of himself, his universe, his relationship to the infinite. They conjure up an elusively complex pattern of religious thought and action.

How strange all this would be to the people who first committed themselves as followers of, disciples to, learners from the carpenter turned teacher of religion and ethics, Jesus of Nazareth. Yet this movement is the spread leaven, the grown mustard plant of his teaching. Many and diverse are the links which connect this movement, or system, or thought pattern, to that small and simple beginning by one who by word, by work, and by what and who he was, revealed the true nature of the Infinite God to finite man.

One of those links is the New Testament—the twenty-seven writings which the early Christians finally agreed upon as the acceptable and authoritative body of Christian writings. Another link is the vast body of Christian writings of the first four centuries which were not accepted as a part of that "acceptable and authoritative" list. Another link is the series of religious groups identifying themselves with this "Christianity," though sometimes called "heretics" by others professing the same identity!

One such link is the group called the "Gnostics." This is the name given to designate those who at least as early as the second century A.D. represented a religious stance, attitude, outlook, philosophy which, while related to the Christian faith, was termed "heretical" by those professing "orthodoxy" as the main stream of Christian thought and expression of that thought.

This book is an approach to the study of this early Christian "heresy" by the connection between three of the above "links"— the New Testament (especially the canonical Gospels and more particularly the Synoptic Gospels), the recently discovered Coptic *Gospel According to Thomas* (a collection of 114 "sayings" attributed to Jesus, about half of them having no parallel in the New Testament), and the Gnostics who owned and used this collection of sayings in the second to fourth centuries as evidenced by the presence of this "Gospel" in the Gnostic library discovered in the mid-1940's at Nag Hammadi in Egypt. Only a few of the fifty writings in that library are currently available for general use. Only since 1959 has the *Gospel According to Thomas* been available for general use. It would be difficult to overestimate its value as a new tool for understanding the very *old* heresy of Gnosticism, the earliest departure from the "faith of the New Testament." In fact, it was a departure from "the faith" before there was a "New Testament" in the canonical sense of the term!

The titles of the four chapters in the first part of the book are definitive and indicate the nature of the study—a search for sources, original forms, authenticity, and theology by comparative study of these 114 "sayings of Jesus" and the canonical Scriptures. The second part of the book presents the *Gospel According to Thomas* and the respective canonical Scripture passages in parallel columns so the reader may make his own comparison as well as follow the discussion presented in the four chapters. To the author's knowledge this has not been done before.

While several translations noted in the documentation have been studied, the translation used here is my own rendering of the Coptic text as arranged, numbered, and presented in the frequently cited book by Guillaumont *et al* and in comparison with the Labib photographic plates of the original text. Students of Coptic will discern places where a rather free paraphrase replaces what would be a rather awkward literal rendering. The canonical parallels, unless otherwise indicated, are quotations from the *New American Standard Version*, which to my mind is the best of the many good translations. It is used with the permission of the Lockman Foundation, La Habra, California.

My indebtedness to many sources will be clearly discerned in the documentation. There is less of this in chapter four where the theological stance of *Thomas* is evaluated. This is due to the necessarily high degree of subjectivism in trying to interpret the meaning of the "sayings" for the gnostic collector and editor of the "sayings" and the gnostic community which evidently valued and used them. In a similar, but perhaps lesser degree, this subjectivism is reflected in chapter three in the "test for authenticity" of the noncanonical "sayings" in *Thomas*. In presenting to my classes the "sayings" which I have come to regard as "most likely authentic sayings of Jesus" I have cautioned them, "Don't look for these sayings in the next edition of the Bible!"

Chapter I

RECENTLY DISCOVERED TEACHINGS OF JESUS
(a quest for sources)

A few years ago a *biblical* cartoon appeared in the *secular* press. Two archaeologists were engaged in their favorite summer pastime, excavation, or, in the language of Zion, "the digs." Their sunburned faces and their distinctive headdress identified them as American archaeologists working in the "Holy Land." One was calling to the other, "Hey, Joe. Come over here. I think I have discovered another commandment!" In seminary circles that was good for many laughs.

No one laughed, however, when, in about 1956, the public press carried the story of the discovery in Egypt of a "Fifth Gospel," one written by the Apostle Thomas. This is one of more than fifty books[1] or "documents" discovered near Nag Hammadi in 1946. They apparently composed the library of a Gnostic community which lived there in or near the ancient village of Chenoboskion in the fourth century. They are in the Coptic language and all are in a good state of preservation for publication.[2] The work of editing and publishing has been and will be a long and tedious process. To date only a very few have been published. The first one to be published appeared in Zurich, Switzerland in 1956 under the Latin title *Evangelium Veritatis*. It is known in English by the translation of Kendrick

---

[1]W. C. van Unnik, *Newly Discovered Gnostic Writings* (Naperville, Ill.: Alec R. Allenson, Inc., 1960), pp. 16-17, gives the complete list of books.
[2]W. C. Till, "New Sayings of Jesus in the Recently Discovered Coptic 'Gospel of Thomas,'" *Bulletin of the John Rylands Library*, XLI (1959), p. 447.

Grobel as *The Gospel of Truth*,³ a Valentinian work.

Another of the Coptic texts was published in Leiden, Holland in 1959 under the Latin title *Evangelium secundum Thomam* and in the same year an English translation of it was published under the title *The Gospel According to Thomas*.⁴ Other English translations⁵ have appeared subsequent to the Guillaumont *et al* publication. It is this "gospel" which was quickly mislabeled "The Fifth Gospel."

It is abundantly clear that it is *not* a "Fifth Gospel" in the sense that Matthew, Mark, Luke, and John are "Gospels." It is *not* by the Apostle Thomas, though it bore his name, just as other noncanonical "gospels" (including a long and well-known childhood narrative of Jesus entitled *The Gospel of Thomas*⁶) bear names of Jesus' first followers, e.g., Peter, Philip, *et al.* This new *Gospel of Thomas* has nothing in common with that childhood narrative. In fact, this newly discovered *Gospel of Thomas* is not all "new" to the world of New Testament scholarship. It is the Coptic version of the Greek "Sayings of Jesus"⁷ discovered in 1897 and 1903 at Oxyrhynchus, Egypt, and studied by every Greek student introduced to the fascinating world of "papyri." The Greek sayings were in some cases rather fragmentary. In fact, one large section was half a sheet of papyrus with the text one would have if he cut a page of printing in half from top to bottom, leaving a half-column.

---

³Kendrick Grobel (trans.), *The Gospel of Truth* (New York: Abingdon Press, 1960.)

⁴A. Guillaumont, H. C. Puech, G. Quispel, W. C. Till, and Y. A. A. Masih, *The Gospel According to Thomas* (New York: Harper and Brothers, 1959.)

⁵Jean Doresse, *The Secret Books of the Egyptian Gnostics* (New York: The Viking Press, 1960), pp. 333-83, and Edgar Hennecke, *New Testament Apocrypha*, ed. W. Schneemelcher (Philadelphia: The Westminster Press, 1963), Vol. I, pp. 511-22. Hereafter cited as Schneemelcher.

⁶Cf. M. R. James, *The Apocryphal New Testament* (Oxford: University Press, 1955); cf. also Schneemelcher, *op. cit.*, pp. 271-338, for a listing of these apocryphal gospels.

⁷For the text of these papyrus sayings in up-to-date sources see Doresse, *op. cit.*, pp. 355-62, where they are placed in juxtaposition with the new Coptic parallels. See also R. M. Grant and D. N. Freedman, *The Secret Sayings of Jesus* (New York: Doubleday and Co., Inc., 1960), pp. 47-56.

The tremendous feature of this new discovery is that the Coptic version is complete, so we now have the full collection of 114 "sayings" and in complete form. A by-product of interest is the indication of how wrong some of the greatest of the Greek scholars had been in their efforts to restore the broken and missing parts of the Greek fragments!

To go back to an earlier statement, no one laughed when the announcement of this discovery was made. The reaction was one of intense excitement, an excitement which has grown as the collection has been studied, an excitement which antici- pates even more fruitful results as the other works are pub- lished, though *The Gospel of Thomas* appears to be the most important by far. It could hardly be otherwise. The pulse of every student of the New Testament must race a bit faster at news that we have 114 *new sayings of Jesus,* even though the announcement must be greatly qualified when the true nature of the work becomes known.

Such a discovery has been hoped for but hardly anticipated. After all, it is a well known fact that the collecting of "sayings of Jesus" started early. Luke indicates that many "gospels" had already been written when he did his research and wrote his Gospel (Luke 1:1-4). It is abundantly clear that there are written sources standing behind and used by Matthew and Luke, and it may be that some such document is also behind Mark (the "Ur-Markus" hypothesis). Paul reflects the circula- tion of a collection of Jesus' sayings when he quotes Jesus that, "It is more blessed to give than to receive" (Acts 20:35), a verse which uninformed students, who have heard that Jesus said it, seek vainly in the canonical Gospels! Paul's frequent references to teachings which he has "from the Lord" may refer, not to "revelations" which he has received in some mystic way, but to Jesus' teachings then in circulation. Study 1 Cor- inthians 7:10, 11:23; 1 Thessalonians 4:15, for example. All these antedate the writing of the canonical Gospels. It is most likely that it is to such a collection that Papias (A.D. 125) re- fers in his well-known dictum that Matthew wrote a "gospel" for the Hebrews. What he describes hardly fits the nature of

our canonical Matthew. Add to all of this the possibility of
other "finds" in light of the Qumran Cave discoveries and one
dares to hope that we may have even more discoveries and
sources for the future.

Exactly what is this new *Gospel of Thomas?* It is a collection
of 114 sayings attributed to Jesus. About half of them are
parallel with sayings in our four canonical Gospels, though
most of them in their expressed form differ greatly from their
canonical parallels. Some of the sayings, a smaller number having no canonical parallels, have been known to us through the
above-mentioned Oxyrhynchus *Logia Jesu.* Still a smaller number have been known to us through their having been quoted
in the writings of early Christian interpreters (Clement of
Alexandria, Irenaeus, Origen, Tertullian, *et al.*), though we
have not known the source of the quotation. At times the early
writer did not know the source. For example, Origen, in a
homily on Jeremiah 3:3, quotes what we now have in *The Gospel of Thomas* as Logion 82.

> He who is near me is near the fire.
> He who is far from me is far from the Kingdom.

Origen says that he has "read somewhere" that Jesus said this.
He questions whether Jesus said it or whether someone with a
faulty memory attributed it to Jesus, but he does use it!

Augustine quoted what we now have as Logion 52.

> His disciples said to him,
>   Twenty-four prophets spoke in Israel
>   and they all spoke about you.
> He said to them,
>   You have dismissed the Living One
>   who is before you and have spoken
>   about the dead.

Augustine confessed ignorance of the source and tossed it off
as coming from "some heretical source," by which he certainly
meant at least "some noncanonical source."

This collection of sayings (logia) is similar to the collection
of sayings (logia) set up by source criticism two generations

ago as a working hypothesis to explain the 272 verses presented *in common* in Matthew and Luke but absent from Mark. The collection known as "Logia,"[8] or "Quelle" (the German word for "source") or simply "Q," was posited as the second major written document used by Matthew and Luke; the first major document was, of course, Mark, since 640 of Mark's 666 verses are used by Matthew and Luke. The "Q" hypothesis was that of just such a collection of sayings as this *Gospel of Thomas.* But, let us hasten to observe, even if such a "Q" collection were possessed and used by Matthew and Luke, the *Gospel of Thomas* is *definitely not it!*

Most of the 114 logia in this collection are merely "sayings," isolated statements with no relation to the context in which they appear. Some are "sayings" which appear to be grouped editorially for reflecting some doctrinal view of the collector. Some are short bits of dialogue between Jesus and some person. Some represent answers which Jesus gave to a question put to him by some person. Many are very fascinating parables, either heretofore unknown parables attributed to Jesus or parables which we have in our Synoptic Gospels, but which are in a much different form and present a much different meaning in the *Gospel of Thomas.* For instance, we may note here and consider in full later that the Synoptic Parable of the Lost Sheep is in the *Gospel of Thomas.* But the collector has either completely misunderstood Jesus' meaning in the parable or has deliberately changed it for a doctrinal purpose. In the Synoptic parable the point is the shepherd's concern over even *one* sheep lost out of *one hundred;* in the *Gospel of Thomas* it is his *best* sheep that is lost and when he finds it he embraces it and assures it, "I love you more than the other sheep because you are the biggest (fattest!) sheep that I have" (Logion 107).

---

[8]A. T. Robertson even wrote a christological study on the content of these verses, *The Christ of the Logia* (Nashville: Sunday School Board of the Southern Baptist Convention, 1924). The hypothesis is clearly and fully presented in such works as B. H. Streeter, *The Four Gospels* (London: Macmillan and Co., Ltd., 1924); V. Taylor, *The Gospels, A Short Introduction* (London: The Epworth Press, 1952); F. C. Grant, *The Gospels: Their Origin and Growth* (New York: Harper and Brothers, 1957).

If there is one single thread which holds the 114 logia together (other than the fact that they are attributed to Jesus)
it is the Gnostic color which runs through the collection like
a ring theme in a Wagner opera! While some of the sayings are
not "Gnostic" in flavor (a few even have "anti-Gnostic" flavor)
they do for the most part reflect Gnostic interest and teachings.

It is definite that the community which owned this library in
Nag Hammadi was Gnostic, much more definite, in fact, than
the once challenged but now little challenged view that the
Qumran community of Dead Sea Scroll fame was Essene.
The presence of this *Gospel of Thomas* in a library of books
which were *absolutely* Gnostic appears to argue for the community acceptance of the Gospel as a Gnostic work. It must
be observed in fairness that one of the most diligent students
of these materials, Gilles Quispel, has argued from the beginning[9] and still does[10] that a possible and perhaps more probable
origin of the book is in some early Jewish-Christian setting
from which the Gnostics received and adopted it and doubtless
altered it to suit their views.

The Gnostics have been called the earliest Christian systematic theologians. Because of prejudiced statements about them
in the Patristic writings, because they were regarded as heretical and dangerous rivals of "orthodox" Christianity in the first
two centuries, because their books were destroyed by the
"orthodox," because we have known them through their much
later writings when their doctrines had faded into the wildest
forms of fantastic speculation, sometimes crude and corrupt
—for all these reasons the Gnostics have been used historically
as a dark backdrop against which to study the brilliance of
some of the Pauline (especially Colossians) and Johannine
(Gospel, First Epistle, Revelation) teachings. While the last
division of this series of studies will be given to the theology
reflected in the *Gospel of Thomas* it should be observed that

---

[9]G. Quispel, "Some Remarks on the Gospel of Thomas," *New Testament
Studies*, Vol. 5, No. 4 (1959).
[10]G. Quispel, "Gnosticism," *Religions in Antiquity Seminar* (Hanover, N. J.:
Dartmouth College Comparative Studies Center, 1966).

the "Gnosticism" reflected in the *Gospel of Thomas* is not all bad; it has some solid Christian values.

Let us come now to address ourselves to the specific subject of this essay, "Recently Discovered Sayings of Jesus, *a quest for sources.*" What are the sources of this enriching find of teachings? They appear to be multiple. The title tells little. Both in the Coptic[11] version and the Greek[12] version (Oxyrhynchus Papyrus, 654) the claim is that these are the "secret words" which the "Living Jesus" spoke and which were recorded by "Didymus Judas Thomas." The expression "secret words" indicates the Gnostic emphasis—these words have "secret" or "hidden" meaning which may be known only by the one who possesses the "gnosis," knowledge. The expression "Living Jesus" is a Gnostic reference to the "Risen Christ" in contrast to the "incarnate Jesus." It may be a typical Gnostic claim that these are post-resurrection "sayings of Jesus" or it may be a Gnostic emphasis on the "Eternal Christ" as the real revealer in contrast to the "incarnate Jesus" who was manifest to the disciples.

Logion 92 definitely supports the idea that Jesus gave no esoteric (secret) teachings until after his resurrection. The Gnostics did not limit the post-resurrection ministry of Jesus to the forty days in Luke-Acts. They held to varying lengths of time between the resurrection and the ascension. In his *Against Heresies,* Irenaeus says that the Valentinian Gnostics taught that this period lasted eighteen months. Gaertner[13] points out that in *Pistis Sophia* the period was eleven years! In the New Testament the Apostle Thomas was called "Didymus," that is, "the twin" (John 11:16, 20:24). *Didymus* is the Greek word for twin just as Thomas (*Thom*) is the Aramaic word for twin. He was a favorite of the Syrian Christians. In several extant apocryphal books he also bore the name "Judas" and was addressed as the twin brother of Jesus, a legend well

---

[11]Guillaumont *et al., op. cit.,* p. 3, Logion 1.

[12]Doresse, *op. cit.,* p. 355, Logion 1.

[13]Bertil Gaertner, *The Theology of the Gospel According to Thomas* (New York: Harper and Brothers, 1961), p. 102.

fixed around Edessa by the third century.[14] He was considered as more enlightened than the other apostles. Logion 13 is a crude parallel of the Caesarea Philippi confession passage of Matthew 16:13-20. There Jesus questions them about the opinions of men concerning him and they answer that men are saying that he is another John the Baptist (fiery preacher of repentance), another Elijah (great miracle worker of God), another Jeremiah (compassionate messenger of God)—he was *like* all of these. When he questions the disciples as to their opinion, Simon Peter confesses him to be the "Christ, the Son of the living God." Jesus accepts this and then commits them to silence on it. In the *Gospel of Thomas* Jesus asks the disciples to "make a comparison" of him with others—very significant in the light of *man's* opinion in the Synoptic account of what he was *like*. Peter answers, "You are like a righteous angel"; Matthew answers, "You are like a wise man of understanding" ("philosopher," literally); Thomas answers, "My mouth cannot say whom you are like." Jesus then answers that he is no longer Thomas' "master" because Thomas has drunk of the stream which flows from Jesus (probably the concept of the Holy Spirit which he would give as a spring of water [John 7:38-39]) and has risen above the "servant" level. He then draws Thomas to one side and gives him *three secret words*[15] which were so meaningful that Thomas could not give them to the *less enlightened* Matthew and Peter lest the words consume them like a fire. If he gave the secret (pronounced the *name?*) they would stone him for blasphemy but anyone who hurt a person who had the "gnosis" would be struck down and consumed by divine fire. To the Gnostics, then, Thomas had the "gnosis" and was a fit recipient and recorder of the revelation of Jesus' *secret words*. The "secret words" or teachings which follow come from various sources.

---

[14]Doresse, *op. cit.*, pp. 337-38, presents an excellent, brief, well-documented review of this legend.

[15]Gaertner, *op. cit.*, pp. 121-25, thinks that the "three words" relate to the "unspeakable name" of Christ, a Gnostic idea. Grant, *op. cit.*, pp. 133-34, also thinks of the three words as related to the secret *Gnostic* name for Jesus.

Other than our canonical Gospels, which will be discussed a bit later, the main sources of the previously known sayings of Jesus now found in the *Gospel of Thomas* are two other apocryphal Gospels known to us already as *The Gospel According to the Hebrews* and *The Gospel According to the Egyptians.*[16] In the early Christian writings, frequent references are made to these Gospels. For example, Clement of Alexandria refers to the *Gospel of the Hebrews* and Jesus' statement, "He that marvels shall reign, and he that has reigned shall rest" (*Stromata* II, 9:45)[17] and a very similar statement in *Stromata* V, 14:96, "He that seeks will not rest until he finds; and he that has found will marvel; and he that has marvelled shall reign; and he that has reigned shall rest." While he does not specifically cite this form as coming from the *Gospel of the Hebrews* it is likely meant to be. It is found as Logion 2 in the *Gospel of Thomas*[18] in a form which may also be translated almost exactly as Clement quoted it except for the absence of the closing clause "and he that has reigned shall rest." The same quotation in Oxyrhynchus 654 is broken but appears to end with the equivalent of the words "and——est" which probably fills out to "and reigning, he shall rest" or "and he shall rest." In any case, the *Gospel According to the Hebrews* appears to be the source of the statement. The working in of the word "rest" gives a Gnostic application to the saying.

In Logion 104 "they" (probably his disciples are meant) urged Jesus to join them in fasting and praying. Jesus responded by asking what sin he had committed that he should fast. He added that there would be plenty of time for fasting when the bridegroom left the bridal chamber. This saying is also found in the *Gospel According to the Hebrews.*[19] A very

---

[16]Cf. James, *op. cit.,* pp. 1-8 (The Gospel According to the Egyptians) and pp. 10-12 (The Gospel According to the Hebrews). See also Schneemelcher, *op. cit.,* pp. 158-78, for partial text, comment, and citation of quotations of these Gospels in the writings of the early interpreters of the Christian faith.

[17]Schneemelcher, *op. cit.,* p. 164.

[18]Guillaumont *et al.* have this as Logion 2; Doresse, as part of Logion 1.

[19]W. C. Till, "New Sayings of Jesus in the Recently Discovered Coptic 'Gospel of Thomas,'" *Bulletin of the John Rylands Library,* XLI (1959), 457.

different saying on the same general theme appears in the Synoptics. It will be treated later.

The Gospel According to the Egyptians includes a part of Logion 22, a very strongly Gnostic saying in which Jesus states that entrance into the kingdom involves the absolute disappearance of all differences, including that of the sexes, "the male will not be male and the female will not be female . . ."[20] There are numerous other *Gospel According to the Egyptians* references but not explicit quotations.

These are examples of possible "sources" of these sayings. Numerous others could be quoted. The fragment of Logion 104 cited above with reference to fasting is also found in *The Gospel of the Nazarenes* which Turner[21] believes may be another form of the *Gospel According to the Hebrews*. Logion 99 may be reflected in a fragment of the *Gospel of the Ebionites* or it may have its source in the Synoptic account of Jesus' mother and brothers coming to seek him during his Galilean ministry. Parallels to different "sayings" found in the Thomas text appear in many early sources. The writers do not indicate the source. Turner[22] cites Puech as holding eighteen passages as a conservative number and then cites others such as Lactantius (Logion 19), Ephraeum Syrus (Logion 30), Irenaeus (Logion 19), and six from Clement of Alexandria. Clement also has other near parallels which may be from Thomas or from the *Gospel of the Egyptians*. All of this presents a complex pattern which, at the present, leaves mostly questions. Were these men quoting some form of Thomas? Were they quoting other "sources" which had also been used by Thomas? More evidence must be found before final answers may be given.

Perhaps the most interesting study of sources relates to the *Gospel of Thomas* parallels with the Synoptic Gospels. Here, too, some basic questions are raised as research guides. Did the collector of the Thomas sayings have our Synoptic Gospels

---

[20]Cf. Till, *ibid.*, and James, *op. cit.*, p. 11.
[21]Hugh Montefiore and H. E. W. Turner, *Thomas and the Evangelists* (Naperville, Illinois: Alec R. Allenson, Inc., 1962), p. 23.
[22]Montefiore and Turner, *op. cit.*, pp. 15-16.

as a "source"? Did he have some "abridged" version of our Synoptic Gospels? Did he and the Synoptic writers have a common source which lies behind all of them?

Only four of the reasonably certain parallels between the Synoptics and the *Gospel of Thomas* are approximately identical. The differences in the others indicate several possibilities: (1) The Synoptics and Thomas had a common source which either one or both of them changed. (2) The Synoptics and Thomas had different sources for these common materials. (3) Thomas has used the Synoptics and has changed them for some theological reason or reasons. A fourth possibility might appear as the opposite of this, i.e., the Synoptics used Thomas and changed the sayings for their theological reasons. This, however, seems impossible since the very earliest suggested date for Thomas as we have it is A.D. 140.[23]

The idea of a Gospel writer changing a saying to suit his theological purpose, or to fit the *Sitz im Leben* of his day has been clearly established. It appears to begin even in the New Testament itself. Luke's "Blessed, ye poor" (6:20) has long been noted as a reflection of Luke's social interest in contrast to Matthew's spiritual interest in "Blessed are the poor in spirit" (5:3). Who changed whom? Or who altered what, in this instance? Dodd[24] and Jeremias[25] have been particularly alert at pointing out instances in which a teaching of Jesus in his own *Sitz im Leben* has been altered in the process of oral transmission to fit a later *Sitz im Leben* in the Christian community, and it is this altered form which appears in the New Testament.

This process was along the same line of usage in which to-

---

[23]This is the date preferred by Puech. See R. M. Wilson, *Studies in the Gospel of Thomas* (London: A. R. Mowbray and Co., Ltd., 1960), pp. 146-47, for summary of opinion on the date.

[24]C. H. Dodd, *The Parables of the Kingdom* (New York: Charles Scribner's Sons, Ltd., 1956).

[25]Joachim Jeremias, *The Parables of Jesus* (New York: Charles Scribner's Sons, Ltd., 1955). Jeremias is particularly suggestive in tracing a parable from the written Gospel back through the church's use to the original setting of Jesus' telling it.

day a teacher or preacher will use a passage of Scripture giving an entirely different application from that of the original teaching. How often Paul's "Whatsoever a man soweth, that shall he also reap" (Gal. 6:7) has been used to warn men of the dread consequences of sin; Paul wrote it as a stewardship passage on generosity or stinginess in paying the preacher of the gospel! How often Jesus' dramatic and moving story of the Rich Man and Lazarus (Luke 16:19-31) has been used to warn men of the torment of hell; Jesus gave it, too, as a stewardship teaching to "money lovers" who thought wealth *per se* meant the favor of God and poverty *per se* meant his disfavor. In a moving experience of response to evangelistic invitation when a father and child or a mother and child have made their commitment to Christ, how often has Isaiah's beautiful "And a little child shall lead them" (Isa. 11:6) been quoted? In its original use it is a reference to a little child safely leading lions and leopards and wolves as pets in Isaiah's dream of the peaceful kingdom which would follow Israel's return from the Babylonian captivity! Such use reflects no intention on the part of the user to do violence to the Scriptures. It is an adaptation for a theological purpose! Such, too, was Paul's radical changing of Psalm 68:18 to meet his need in writing Ephesians 4:8. How much this was done in the life of the early church is clear in comparing such a work as Thomas with the Synoptic Gospels. We do well to recall, too, that the process of canonization, of determining which would be considered as the "authoritative" Christian writings, was in progress right on up to A.D. 397 and the Council of Carthage. Only after that can we speak of the Christians as having a "New Testament."

The question of sources where Thomas and the Synoptics are concerned requires some comparison and contrast in their parallels. The differences follow several well-defined lines. As a working basis (not to determine "conclusions" before the "evidence" is in!) let us assume the *priority* of the Synoptics and *their use* by Thomas. Difference may be noted along these lines: Thomas' *additions* to the Synoptics; Thomas' *deletions* from the Synoptics; Thomas' *conflation* of several Synoptic sayings into one saying; Thomas' *changes* of an entire saying.

Additions

Montefiore[26] uses the term "embellishment" for some examples of this type of change. In some ways this may be more accurate, a "dressing up" of the saying with the result that it is more colorful, more descriptive. In other ways, however, the "embellishments" appear to be "additions" for a definite theological bias on the part of the collector. Consider only a representative few of these changes; the list could be a long one.

Logion 107 has already been cited in this study as an illustration of Thomas' changed form of a Synoptic saying. This is the Parable of the Lost Sheep. In Matthew 18:12-14 this story is used by Jesus to illustrate the importance of the children who were coming to him, God's concern for them, the danger of casting a stumbling stone in the way of one of them. In Luke 15:3-7 it is the first of three parables (Lost Sheep, Lost Coin, Lost Son) to illustrate God's concern for even one person. The setting was that in which the Pharisees and scribes were grumbling because Jesus was associating with sinners. Jesus told the story to show that he represented a God who cared for *every single person* regardless of external conditions.

In Luke it is not in any way a "kingdom" parable; in Matthew the passage starts out on a "greatness in the kingdom" note but seems to depart from that as a primary emphasis. In Thomas' Logion 107 it is a "kingdom" parable like the Synoptic kingdom parables in Matthew 13 and parallels. In Thomas, the shepherd tires himself out seeking the lost sheep because it is the largest (fattest) one he has. Whereas in the Synoptics the shepherd calls in his neighbors and asks that they rejoice with him, in Thomas he addresses his joy to the sheep, assuring it, "I love you beyond (more than, or above) the ninety-and-nine." The reason is obvious—it is his choice sheep. Grant[27] seems to be correct in rejecting the suggestion that the shep-

---

[26]Montefiore, *op. cit.*, pp. 48-52.
[27]Grant, *op. cit.*, p. 193.

herd wanted the sheep simply to fill out the incomplete number 99; that he wanted his flock to be 99 + 1, or the perfect 100. This is the reason for his seeking the sheep in the more mystical Gnostic work *The Gospel of Truth*.[28] Others appear to be on the right track in seeing here an addition for a Gnostic purpose. The "largest" sheep, the one preferred "above" or "beyond" the others is the one which has the "gnosis." Thomas' addition of the "largest" idea completely changes the thrust of the Synoptic idea—God's care for *every* person.

A similar addition in the Mustard Seed parable (Matt. 13:33-35) gives a Gnostic coloration. This is Logion 20. The disciples ask Jesus to tell them what the kingdom of heaven is like. This definitely suggests a Matthean influence by using the word "heaven"; Thomas' regular formula is "kingdom of the Father." The remainder of the parable is almost identical with Matthew except for the additional emphasis that the mustard seed fell on "tilled soil," hence, the Gnostic force. It is the prepared, enlightened one who produces fruit, i.e., the one who has the "gnosis."

Logion 100 has an interesting addition which does not appear to have a Gnostic overtone. It is the teaching of Jesus on rendering to God and to Caesar their respective due (Matt. 22:16-21 and parallels). There is no indication in Thomas (as there is in the Synoptics) that those who asked Jesus the question were trying to trap him. "They" (the people? the disciples?) brought to Jesus a gold coin (rather than his requesting it). They said simply, "Caesar's officers request taxes from us." It is an implied question. Jesus responds,

> Give to Caesar Caesar's things;
> Give to God God's things;
> Give to me my things.

---

[28]It is most interesting that in *The Gospel of Truth* (32:1-30), it was the *Sabbath* on which the shepherd labored to find the sheep, thus showing that one must work to bring about salvation ("gnosis") even on the Sabbath; it is a day of salvation.

The addition of the third category most exactly fits Jesus' situation in confrontation with a people who held tenaciously to *loyalty* to God but refused to subscribe *loyalty* to him.[29] If he said it, it is difficult to see how the Synoptic writers omitted it. The conclusion would be that they simply did not have it.

Deletions

In the category of Thomas' Logia which have experienced deletion from a more detailed (or longer) Synoptic account, consider a few examples.

Logion 90 (parallel, Matt. 11:28-30) is a good one.

Logion 90	Matthew 11:28-30
Come to me,	Come to Me, all who are weary and heavy laden, and I will give you rest.
	Take My yoke upon you, and learn from Me, for I am gentle and humble in heart; and you shall
because my yoke is easy, my lordship gentle, and you shall find for yourselves, rest.	find rest for your souls.
	For My yoke is easy, and My load is light.

The Gnostic dislike of the idea of a relationship to Jesus as a "burden" prompts Thomas to delete the "weary and heavy laden" expression (Matthew 11:28), to delete "load" in Matthew 11:30 and to replace it with the rather beautifully expressed "my lordship is gentle."[30] He also reverses the order (another type of change) so the promised "rest" comes as the ultimate climax. "Rest" was one of the favorite Gnostic concepts of the state to which the possessor of "gnosis" came.

Logion 63 is very radically different from its parallel in Luke 12:16-21, the Parable of the Rich Fool. It is the deletion,

---

[29]See Gaertner, *op. cit.*, p. 33 for a radically different and definitely Gnostic explanation of this addition.

[30]If he is using Matthew rather than their using a common source. See H. D. Betz, "The Logion of the Easy Yoke and the Rest," *Journal of Biblical Literature*, LXXXVI, Part I (March, 1967), 10-24.

however, which is most remarkable. In Luke the Fool is a farmer; in Thomas the Fool is a merchant who invests his money
in a farm project. In both he becomes very wealthy. In both
he considers his material possessions with no consciousness of
his spiritual bankruptcy. In both he dies very suddenly. In
Luke there is a God-pronounced sentence of doom. This is
absent in the Thomas account. In the omission there is a loss
of colorful *detail* as well as a loss of warning that God cares
more for man's spiritual than for his material status. That would
have been an excellent "Gnostic" emphasis. Did Thomas change
Luke, or did he not have Luke?

Logion 57 (Matt. 13:24-30, 36-43) is an interesting contrast
which raises a multitude of problems, the Parable of the Wheat
and the Tares. It requires approximately 170 words to get
Matthew's Greek version into English; Thomas' Coptic version
can be easily expressed in 70 to 75. The dialogue between the
master and the servants relative to the source of the tares is
missing; the master simply instructs the workers to leave the
tares until harvest time. The harvest scene is greatly shortened.
The most noticeable omission is the entire allegorizing explanation of the parable which was directed to the disciples in the
absence of the multitude.

Montefiore[31] has a most fruitful and suggestive treatment of
the almost absolute absence in Thomas of the allegorizing materials in the Synoptics. His concluding suggestions are, in the
main, two: (1) Thomas had a more primitive source than the
Synoptics, one lacking much of the allegorizing which Jeremias
and the others have concluded to be the later work of the
church. (2) Thomas preferred to omit the allegorizing explanation and leave the "secret" meaning of the parable for
only those who had the "gnosis" to understand. His overwork-
ing of Jesus' "Let him who has ears to hear, hear" underlines
his view of the teachings as being esoteric in nature.

---

[31]Montefiore, *op. cit.*, pp. 60-64.

Conflation

Both Gaertner[32] and Montefiore[33] have done most helpful groundwork in the area of Thomas' practice of taking parts of often widely separated Synoptic teachings and combining them into one new passage. Sometimes the result leaves one a bit puzzled as to Thomas' purpose or intended teaching. At other times the teaching is clear.

This reminds one of rather simple or naive conflations by one who spontaneously and from a faulty memory quotes passages out of context in "proof-text" support of some idea. Or the irreverent delight we had as intermediate boys in a "favorite Scripture" quoting session in Sunday School when two or three in series would inevitably come up with such a "conflation" as,

> "Judas went out and hanged himself."
> "Go thou and do likewise."
> "What thou doest, do quickly."

We did not know the scholarly tradition in which we stood! Observe the conflation in Logion 33.

> Jesus said,
> "What you hear in one ear and in the other,
>   proclaim from your housetops[34]
> Because no one lights a lamp
>   and puts it under a bushel
>   nor in a concealing place,
>   but he sets it on the lampstand
>   so all who enter or leave
>   may see its light.

This combines elements of Matthew 10:27—Luke 12:3; Mark 4:21—Luke 8:16; Matthew 5:15—Luke 11:33. It is a masterful job of interweave so the parts are almost beyond identifica-

---

[32]Gaertner, *op. cit.*, pp. 35-43.
[33]Montefiore, *op. cit.*, pp. 71-73.
[34]A *very* non-Gnostic emphasis! There would be nothing "secret" about such a transmission of knowledge.

tion. This was a frequently used technique of the Gnostics and
helps to put Thomas into that milieu.

Logion 39 is a simpler conflation of Matthew 23:13, Luke
11:52, and Matthew 10:16.

> Jesus said,
> The Pharisee and the scribe have
>   received the keys of understanding;
>   they have hidden them;
>   they did not [enter?]
>   nor did they let those who wished [enter?].
> But you, become wise as serpents
>   and innocent as doves.

The first saying is a charge against the Pharisees and scribes in
both Thomas and the Synoptics. The second saying is, in the
Synoptics, a charge to the disciples that in their conflict with
men as they proclaim the kingdom message they shall be as
wise as serpents in avoiding danger, but as harmless as doves
in retaliation or striking back. In Thomas this is lost. The saying is merely a warning against the Pharisees. Probably it is
the idea of "knowledge" that has caused the conflation; both
"gnosis" and "phronesis" are in the sayings.

A similar hortatory purpose has led Thomas to combine
parts of Matthew 13:45-46, 13:44, 6:19-20—Luke 12:33 in
Logion 76.

> Jesus said,
> The kingdom of the Father is like a
>   man who was a merchant carrying
>   his merchandise. He found a pearl.
>   He was a wise merchant. He
>   sold his merchandise; he
>   bought the pearl for himself.
> You, also, seek for the treasure
>   which does not become valueless,
>   which does not wear out,
>   in the place where no moth
>   can come to devour, and no
>   worm to destroy.

The form changes of the Synoptic Parable of the Pearl of Great Price are obvious and significant, especially for a Gnostic, i.e., the lowly merchant who is wise enough to receive the "gnosis" gives up his merchandising for the higher and eternal treasure. Is the treasure "gnosis" or "Christ" as in the Synoptic account? The exhortation to seek the eternal and secure treaure is a natural combination.

Changes

For present purpose let two examples suffice to illustrate logia in Thomas which are completely different from the Synoptic parallel both in form and meaning.

Logion 13, which in part roughly parallels Matthew 16:13-16 (with parallels in Mark 8:27-30 and Luke 9:18-21), in part is different and has large additions. It has been observed earlier in this essay. In Thomas both Matthew and Peter make a "Great Confession" but Jesus is not pleased with them. Thomas then makes a "Great Confession" which Jesus accepts, for which he commends Thomas, and because of which he trusts to him the three unutterable words. The purpose of this logion is clear—it identifies Thomas as the most enlightened of the disciples and the one who can best be the revealer of Jesus.

Logion 14 is both change and conflation. It combines elements of Jesus' teachings on giving, praying, and fasting (Matt. 6:1-18) with his instructions when the disciples were sent out to preach (Luke 10:8-9—Matt. 10:8), and his teachings on what really defiles one spiritually (Matt. 15:11—Mark 7:15). There is even a touch of 1 Corinthians 10:27 in the "eat what is set before you" statement!

The main point of interest is that in the Matthew 6:1-18 passage Jesus anticipates that his disciples will give alms, pray, and fast as expressions of their religious devotion. He tells them to avoid play-acting pretense (the meaning of "hypocrite") and do these things as genuine acts of worship. In the Thomas passage he makes no such assumption about their giving, praying, and fasting, and states categorically that to lo these things is to involve one's self in "sin," "condemnation," and "doing evil" to one's "spirit." This suggests an absolute rejection of recognized *forms* of worship and a withdrawal from society. In such case one is to understand that wherever he goes in his ministry among men (healing) he may accept whatever food is offered him without fear of being defiled since spiritual defilement is not a matter of what goes into one's mouth but of what is already inside of one. Its defiling nature is evident even in the words (teachings?) which come from one's mouth. This last is very much like the spirit of Jesus' teachings. The first part is a Gnostic rejection of formal worship.

Conclusions

What conclusions relative to *sources* used by Thomas may be drawn from such analysis as this? They must be in part tentative. They fall along these lines:

1. It appears definite that the Synoptic writers did not have Thomas, certainly not in the form in which we now have it.

2. It appears fairly certain that Thomas did not have the Synoptics in the full form in which we now have them. He does appear to have had a shorter form of the "sayings" passages in Matthew and Luke. It can be argued that he did not have such a source, but rather that both he and the Synoptics had a common source which they used in different ways, with different guiding principles.

3. It appears fairly certain that Thomas had an independent source which the Synoptics did not have. If they had it, they rejected it as unreliable even though some of the sayings recommend themselves as being genuine. The reliability of this independent source is debated today. Quispel[35] has great confidence in it. Gaertner[36] and Grant are much more cautious. In fact, Grant states in a rather total look at Thomas that "the *Gospel of Thomas* contains, not what Jesus said, but what certain men *wished* he had said!"[37]

---

[35]Quispel, *opp. cit.* Both articles have this optimistic outlook.
[36]Gaertner, *op. cit.*, p. 54.
[37]Grant and Freedman, *op. cit.*, p. 20.

Chapter II

RECENTLY DISCOVERED PARABLES OF JESUS
(a quest for original forms)

When one thinks of the teachings of Jesus he thinks immediately of the parables. There is such a minimum of this form in the larger *Mashal* type of teaching in the Old Testament, and so few relatively are acquainted with the parabolic content of rabbinical teaching that Jesus' use of parables is thought to be absolutely unique. Too, they are found only in the Synoptic Gospels. There appear to be "acted parables" in the Fourth Gospel and there may be miracle stories known in other traditions as parable stories, but parables *as such* are not in the Fourth Gospel.

As indicated in the last chapter Dodd[1] and Jeremias[2] have pointed out the evidences that in some cases the Synoptic parables appear in an adaptation to a later setting in the church rather than in the original setting in which Jesus gave them. For this later setting the form of the parable has been changed. This started rather early in the church even if one takes the rather generally accepted later date (A.D. 80-85) for the writing of Matthew and Luke. It started much earlier, of course, if Harnack[3] is right in dating these books earlier (A.D. 60-65).

---

[1]Dodd, *op. cit.*, pp. 124ff., for example.
[2]Jeremias, *op. cit.*, pp. 55ff., for example.
[3]Adolph Harnack, *The Date of Acts and The Synoptic Gospels* (New York: G. P. Putnam's Sons, 1911).

What light does the *Gospel of Thomas* throw on this procedure? The answer to that question depends in part on the answer to another question, "Which has the original form, Thomas or the Synoptics?," or yet another question, "Does Thomas have the original form or do the Synoptics have the original form, or have *both* of them changed an earlier traditional form so the parable appears in the new form?" It is in search of the answers to these questions that we embark on *a quest for original forms.* All writers approach this question cautiously; some feel that we cannot, at this stage of study, find answers; we can only raise questions.

Let us divide the examination into two categories: *Parabolic Sayings* and *Parabolic Stories.* We will follow the order of Thomas. First, we will examine some—

Parabolic Sayings

Logion 14, the last sentence, has a parallel in Matthew 15:11 and Mark 7:15. While not in parable story form it is called a "parable" in Matthew by the disciples and in Mark by the "people." It is easy to see how a "story" could have been built upon it.

Logion 14d	Matt. 15:11	Mark 7:15
Because what goes into your mouth will not defile you, but what comes out of your mouth.	Not what enters into the mouth defiles the man, but what proceeds out of the mouth, this defiles the man.	There is nothing outside the man which going into him can defile him; but the things which proceed out of the man are what defile the man.

A comparative study of these suggests that Mark most likely has the original form. Matthew has condensed and simplified it. Thomas has almost exactly the Matthew version. The difference here, then, is largely a matter of setting. Matthew and Mark appear to have the original setting in a dialogue between Jesus and the Pharisees on what really constitutes defilement—the outer and physical, or the inner and spiritual? Thomas has taken over both the saying and the meaning but has put it into a different setting—Jesus' instructions to his disciples as they go out "into the world" to serve him.

Logion 21 is a rather long saying on the nature of discipleship. Embedded in it is an almost exact quotation of Matthew 24:43.

Logion 21	Matt. 24:43
If the master of the house knows that the thief is coming, he will stay awake until he comes and will not permit him to dig through his kingdom house to carry away his goods.	. . . if the head of the house had known at what time of the night the thief was coming, he would have been on the alert and would not have allowed his house to be broken into.

While the saying in Logion 21 is almost identical with Matthew's version, it has been "colored up" a bit by the use of the word "kingdom" and by the closing emphasis on not letting the goods be stolen. This, plus the fact of a different setting, indicates that Matthew has the original form and setting in a warning with reference to the coming of the Son of Man. Thomas has changed it to fit a new setting in a teaching on the discipleship of the true "Gnostic" including a warning to watch out for "the world." This is the real threat to one who has the "gnosis." He does not worry about some apocalyptic "coming" of the Son of Man. There is no place in his system for that. He worries about the threat imposed by "the world," the material *kosmos* which is his enemy.

Logion 26 parallels the familiar Matthew 7:3-5 "mote and beam" passage. The major difference is one of verb tense and mood.

Logion 26	Matt. 7:3-5
Jesus said, The speck which is in your brother's eye you see, but the log which is in your own eye you do not see.	And why do you look at the speck in your brother's eye, but do not notice the log that is in your own eye? v. 3 Or how can you say to your brother, 'Let me take the speck out of your eye', and behold, the log is in your own eye? v. 4 You hypocrite, first take the log
When you cast the log out of	out of your own eye; and then

| your own eye, then you will see clearly to cast the speck out of your brother's eye. | you will see clearly *enough* to take the speck out of your brother's eye.   v. 5 |

The differences are obvious. The Logion 26 statement almost exactly parallels Matthew's verse 3 and verse 5. In between Matthew has verse 4 which has no parallel in Thomas. In Logion 26 both parts of the saying are simple declarative statements. In Matthew the first two parts are *interrogative* and the third is *imperative.* The context of Logion 26 helps little; it is in a series of short logia and its only contextual connection is with Logion 25 which is an admonition on brother love. In Matthew the entire context relates to a hypercritical attitude toward one's brother. Two solutions appear: (1) Both Thomas and Matthew have used a common source to which Matthew has added the dramatic question in v. 4. (2) Thomas has deleted the question in v. 4 as superfluous for carrying forward the teaching. Knowing Thomas' inclination for condensing, this may appear the more likely. However, knowing Matthew's liking for the *dramatic* and *didactic,* the former solution is more attractive.

Logion 31 strikes a most familiar chord. It has its parallel in Matthew 13:57; Mark 6:4; Luke 4:23-24; and John 4:44.

Logion 31	Synoptics and John
No prophet is acceptable in his village,	. . . A prophet is not without honor except in his home town, and in his *own* household. (Matt.) . . . A prophet is not without honor except in his home town and among his *own* relatives and in his *own* house. (Mark) . . . no prophet is welcome in his home town. (Luke v. 24) . . . a prophet has no honor in his own country. (John)
no physician heals those who know him.	. . . No doubt you will quote this proverb to Me, 'Physician, heal yourself . . .' (Luke v. 23)

Since Thomas reflects so very little likelihood of having John's Gospel it seems that John as a source may be ruled out here. Both Matthew and Luke have condensed Mark's statement deleting "among his own kin" and Luke has also deleted "in his own house"; Matthew retains it. Comparison of Luke and Logion 31 shows that they are almost exactly the same, even to adding the "physician" part of the proverb lacking in Matthew, Mark, and John. It appears, then, that in this case that Thomas and Luke have a common source not possessed by the other Gospels, or Thomas has used Luke as the original source of the "physician" proverb. One wonders if the fact (Col. 4:14) that Luke himself was a physician accounted for his possession of this "physician" proverb unknown to the others!

Logion 45 is another example of conflation. It brings together the "fruit" passage from the Sermon on the Mount (Matt. 7:16; Luke 6:43) and the "corrupt speech" passages of Matthew 12:34-35, and Luke 6:45.

Logion 45	Synoptics
They do not gather grapes from thorns, nor do they gather figs from thistles because they produce no fruit.	. . . Grapes are not gathered from thornbushes, nor figs from thistles, are they? (Matt. 7:16) . . . For men do not gather figs from thorns, nor do they pick grapes from a briar bush. (Luke 6:44)
A good man brings forth good out of his treasure, an evil man brings forth evil out of his treasure which is in his heart and speaks evil things. Because out of the abundance of the heart he brings forth evil things.	The good man out of *his* good treasure brings forth what is good; and the evil man out of *his* evil treasure brings forth what is evil. (Matt. 12:35) [Luke's statement is identical with Matthew's except that he adds,] . . . for his mouth speaks from that which fills his heart. (Luke 6:45)

When a comparison is made of the total contextual settings of all three the impression is almost overwhelming that Thomas had both Matthew and Luke and that he took from both what he needed. Here are the reasons. Both Matthew and Thomas

have the "grapes . . . figs" order. Thomas chose this over Luke's
"figs . . . grapes" order. In both Thomas and Matthew in the
second part of the saying which relates to the "treasure of a
man's heart" the setting is of blasphemy against the Holy
Spirit; but not in Luke. Thomas seems to have used Matthew all the way except to pick up Luke's closing statement
not found in Matthew, "His mouth speaks from that which fills
his heart." Thomas applies this to the evil of speaking blasphemy against the Holy Spirit. Luke used it only in a general
way to show that one's true inner nature is evident even in
his spoken words.

Logion 47 presents a non-Synoptic parabolic (or wisdom)
saying and then adds a conflation of materials from Matthew
and Luke. The result is a fascinating interweave.

Logion 47	Synoptics
It is not possible for a man to ride two horses and to stretch two bows, and it is not possible for a servant to serve two masters, or he will honor one and offend the other.	No one can serve two masters; for either he will hate the one and love the other, or he will hold to one and despise the other. You cannot serve God and Mammon. [Matthew 6:24 and Luke 16:13 are practically identical.]
No one drinks old wine and immediately desires to drink new wine.	And no one, after drinking old *wine* wishes for new; for he says, 'The old is good *enough.*' (Luke 5:39)
They do not put new wine into old wineskins lest they burst,	And no one puts new wine into old wine-skins; otherwise the new wine will burst the skins, and it will be spilled out, and the skins will be ruined. But new wine must be put into fresh wine-skins. (Luke 5:37-38)
and they do not put old wine into new wineskins, lest it spoil them. They do not sew an old patch on a new garment, lest there would come a tear.	. . . No one tears a piece from a new garment and puts it on an old garment; otherwise he will both tear the new, and the piece from the new will not match the old. (Luke 5:36)

... the patch pulls away from the
garment, and a worse tear results.
(Matt. 9:16) [Mark 2:21 is little
different from Matthew.]

The idea in the first part of the Thomas saying is that a person must decide what course he will take in life. To try to follow the true "gnosis" and at the same time follow the material world is as impossible as riding two horses going in opposite directions; or drawing two bows to shoot two arrows at two separate targets; or being a slave to two masters simultaneously! The first two illustrations are noncanonical sayings but, because they fit so exactly and are so perfectly matched with the third, they commend themselves as authentic words from Jesus. The differences between the Synoptics and Thomas on the "servant . . . master" passage and the addition of the two new sayings point to a source other than the Synoptics.

In the second part of the logion when Thomas speaks of the "new wine" and the "patched" garments, his sayings are so different from the Synoptics both in content and order that it is difficult to think of his using them. It appears more likely that they have here a common source and have used it differently. If Thomas is using the Synoptics it appears that he is more inclined to Luke's version than to Matthew and Mark, even though his order is radically different from Luke.

Logion 47 order	Luke's order
	No one puts a *new* patch on an *old* garment.
No one drinks old wine and then desires new.	No one drinks old wine and then desires new.
No one puts new wine into old wineskins.	No one puts new wine into old wineskins.
No one puts old wine into new wineskins.	New wine must be put into new wineskins.
No one puts an old patch on a new garment.	

In comparison, note these differences: (1) Luke's order has *first* the tearing of a *new* piece of cloth so as to patch an *old* garment with the result that both garments are injured; Thomas' order has *last* the sewing of an *old* patch on a new garment. One will be injured but which one it is, is not clear, the old garment from which the patch is taken or the new garment to which it is sewn. (2) Luke speaks of the necessity of putting *new* wine into *new* wineskins; Thomas speaks of *not* putting *old* wine into *new* wineskins. Otherwise they parallel each other even to the including of a reference to one's not desiring new wine after drinking old wine, a reference not found in Matthew and Mark. In Luke it may be that Jesus is rebuking his hearers for their unwillingness to give up the "old wine," Judaism, and to accept the "new wine" which he offers. There is in Thomas an interesting *chiasmos* which is not in Luke's account:

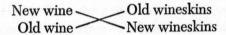

This concept of Christianity as "new wine" must have meant much to the early church. Here in the three Synoptics and in Thomas it is found in differing expressions of a *parabolic* teaching. In John 2:1-10 it appears as a *miracle* story. It must be the same. In both the Synoptics and John it is in a "wedding" setting. In both it points up the superiority of what Christ is offering to that which is found in Judaism. In both the idea is present that this "new wine" cannot be contained by the "old forms" (wineskins in the Synoptics; earthen jars in John) of Judaism. In the process of oral transmission: Did it "grow" from a "parabolic" teaching in the Synoptic tradition to a "miracle" teaching in the Johannine tradition? Did it "reduce" from a "miracle" teaching in one tradition to a "parable" teaching in the other? Was the "parabolic teaching" given on the occasion of the "miracle teaching" with one line of oral transmission preserving the "parabolic teaching" and the other the "miracle teaching"? Or to be very comprehensive, are two separate occasions represented in the two accounts with the "parabolic teaching" growing out of one and the "miracle teaching" growing out of the other?

A similar survey of *all* the parabolic sayings in Thomas leads to the same tentative conclusion reached in this partial survey, i.e., in the great majority of cases it appears that the Synoptics have the *original form* of the teaching. In only a few does it appear that Thomas may have the original form and this seems almost impossible to "prove."

Parabolic Stories

When one turns to the parabolic stories in Thomas, he is in one of the most fascinating areas of the work. In this study a selected number of the parables will be used and only those with Synoptic parallels. The next division of the study will give attention to non-Synoptic parables.

A good starting point may be with the parables in Matthew 13:1-52. Frequently writers state that all the parables in Matthew 13 are found in Thomas. If this is true, it appears that these writers do not consider the beautiful little one-sentence parable about the *scribe* who becomes a *kingdom disciple* and discovers that he has not lost his *old* treasure (Torah) but has added to it a *new* treasure (Christ). It appears to be a parable but is not one of the "kingdom" parables (Matt. 13:52).

It is instructive to note the difference in the *order* of these parables in:

Matthew 13	Logion
The Parable of the Sower, 3-8, (19-23)[4]	9
The Parable of the Tares, 24-30 (36-43)[5]	57
The Parable of the Mustard Seed, 31-32	20
The Parable of the Leaven, 33-35	96
The Parable of the Hid Treasure, 44	109
The Parable of the Pearl, 45-46	76
The Parable of the Net, 47-50	8

[4-5]The parenthesis indicates the allegorizing explanation of the parables. Thomas omits it.

In Matthew these "kingdom" parables stand together in dramatic force. In Thomas they are widely scattered and appear in most cases to have no contextual reason for their position. This suggests that in Thomas' source or sources these were isolated sayings which had been preserved. It suggests that Matthew's source probably had them as isolated sayings and that he has grouped them for his definite *didactic* purpose just as in Matthew 8-9 he grouped a large number of miracles to show Jesus' power over inanimate forces of nature, over sicknesses of all kind, over spiritual malady, and even over death. Thomas' scattered presentation and the differences in detail and thrust in some of them suggest an independent source, or a common source with Matthew, which source Thomas has changed to suit his theological purpose.

The Parable of the Sower (Matt. 13:3-8; Logion 9) does not differ greatly in the two accounts. Thomas' detail of the sower *filling his hand* and sowing adds a dramatic and perhaps authentic touch. His reference to some seed falling "on the road" is clearer than Matthew's "beside the road." The reference is to the small paths that wound through the wheat fields. In "broadcast" sowing some seed would fall there. In Matthew the seed which fell on rocky soil sprouted but was scorched by the heat of the sun; in Thomas it simply got no root and produced no fruit. In Matthew the seed which fell among thorns grew but the thorns choked it out so it bore no fruit; in Thomas the thorns choked the seed and the worms ate "them" (seed or plants?). In Matthew the seed on good soil bore fruit; some one hundred to one, some sixty to one, and some thirty to one in descending anticlimax. In Thomas it bore sixty to one, and double that—one hundred twenty to one in climactic order. In Matthew it is a kingdom parable; in Thomas it is not. In Matthew, in response to the request of the disciples, Jesus gave a lengthy allegorizing explanation of the parable. In Thomas no application whatever is made. One who had the "gnosis" might possibly relate it to the *action* involved in Gnosticism and to the idea that the one with the true "gnosis" bears fruit. Thomas may have omitted the allegorizing explanation because of the

Gnostic's dislike for allegorizing. Or his source may have been an early and/or shorter form lacking the allegory.

The Parable of the Tares (Matt. 13:24-30; Logion 57) is far inferior in Thomas. Just how much shorter it is was considered in the first chapter. The Matthew passage is rich in detail; Thomas has an absolute minimum of detail. Either he had a separate source or he simply condensed Matthew's account almost to an absurdity. He may not have had the allegorizing explanation (Matt. 13:36-43) relating the parable to the end of the world, the judgment separating "wheat from tares," the eternal burning, etc. He may have had it but rejected it because the Gnostic had *little* use for allegorizing and *no* use for the kind of eschatology reflected in the explanation. Grant[6] suggests that he omitted it simply because he had *his own* explanation of its meaning! An esoteric one, no doubt! Matthew is far superior here.

The Parable of the Mustard Seed (Matt. 13:31-32; Logion 20) seems definitely to be derived from the Synoptics. It even has the Matthean "kingdom of heaven" introduction in contrast to Thomas' favored "kingdom of the Father." Too, in the Markan version this parable is introduced by a question (by Jesus) and in Thomas it is introduced by a question (by the disciples). This is a rare form.

The only major detail which differs is that in Thomas the mustard seed falls on *ploughed* ground. This is probably[7] a Gnostic reference to the one who is prepared by the "gnosis" to receive the kingdom. In both Synoptics and Thomas the major interest is in the almost infinitesimal size of the seed and the tremendous plant which results from the sowing.

The Parable of the Leaven (Matt. 13:33-35; Logion 96) is another which seems to be derived by Thomas from a separate source. It is a "kingdom of the Father" parable in contrast to

---

[6]Grant, *op. cit.*, p. 165.

[7]This idea that "ploughed" ground in Thomas reflects a Gnostic emphasis may have been unduly stressed. The central thrust of the earlier Synoptic parable is that the result of sowing depends upon the *condition* of the ground (Matt. 13:3-8, 19-23).

"kingdom of heaven" in Matthew. In it a woman places leaven in meal to make bread. The parable has striking contrasts to be so short.

Thomas	Matthew
The kingdom is like a woman.	The kingdom is like leaven.
It is a *little* leaven.	It is simply leaven.
It is placed in dough.	It is placed in three measures of meal.
The woman makes large loaves.	The leaven spreads to permeate the meal.

Grant[8] notes that Thomas compares the kingdom with a *woman*, but Matthew compares it with *leaven*. It sounds as if that is right but one wonders if the comparison is not with the *action* in both. The kingdom is like *what happens when* . . . etc. It is true that Thomas' emphasis is on the *human action* (even if it was a woman!)[9] whereas, in Matthew the leaven by its own nature spreads. In both instances it is the "small to large" nature of the kingdom which is in focus.

The Parable of the Hid Treasure (Matt. 13:44; Logion 109) is very different in the Matthew and Thomas accounts.

Thomas	Matthew
Jesus said, The kingdom is like a man who had a treasure in his field, without knowing it.	The kingdom of heaven is like a treasure hidden in a field; which a man found and hid again.
And he died; he left it to his son. The son did not know; he received the field and then sold it.	In his joy he went and sold all he had and bought that field.
He who purchased it went and while plowing found the treasure.	(Author's translation)
He began to lend money to anyone he wished.	

[8]Grant, *op. cit.*, p. 187.
[9]The very fact that a *woman* is used as the "heroine" indicates authenticity since a Gnostic would never create a story with a woman as the central figure and in a favorable light. Women were held in low regard by the Gnostics.

In Thomas' account the original owner did not know about the treasure; in Matthew's account also this appears to be true but it is not expressly stated. In Thomas' account the field passed to the third owner who accidentally discovered his treasure. In Matthew the second man discovered the treasure, recognized the value, converted everything he had to cash in order to buy the field and joyfully to possess the treasure— simply having it was joy. In Thomas' account the owner-finder enters the investment business immediately!

In Matthew's use and setting the meaning of the parable is clear. The kingdom is the greatest treasure one may possess and one must give it such priority that he will give up everything in order to possess it. This was the lesson in the Parable of the Pearl both in Matthew and Thomas (where the pearl may be Christ or it may be the "gnosis"). There does not seem to be a clear meaning in Thomas' Parable of the Hid Treasure. It hardly has a Gnostic force since it ends with the farmer becoming an investment lender. This would be a low and undesirable position in the mind of the Gnostic and Logion 95 forbids lending at interest. Perhaps it is a subtle warning against a careless attitude which may cause one to overlook a treasure which is right before him.

The Parable of the Pearl (Matt. 13:45-46; Logion 76) has been discussed earlier.[10] Thomas' version seems to be taken directly from the Synoptic account and to have the same meaning—the prior importance of the kingdom, or the "gnosis," or Christ. It closes with a reference to the imperishable treasure.

The Parable of the Net (Matt. 13:47-50; Logion 8), too, appears to be taken from the Synoptic account. It is different enough, however, to point to some other source. In the Matthew account the plural "they" is used; in the Thomas account only one "man" is used and he is called a "wise fisherman." The word "fisherman" in Thomas has a more authentic sound where fishing is involved than the indefinite "they" in Matthew's account. The word "wise" in Thomas (absent in Matthew) is

---

[10]*Supra,* p. 30.

definitely a Gnostic color word lending a less authentic sound to his account.

In Matthew's version the nets encompassed all kinds of fish—good and bad. In Thomas nothing is said about "bad" fish; the net encompasses many *small* fish and among them is one *large* fish. Without a second thought the wise fisherman returned the *small* fish to the sea and kept the *large* one. In Matthew this is a "last judgment" parable in which the good fish represent the righteous, the bad fish represent the wicked, the separation is at the end of the world. Thomas' account has been thoroughly gnosticized. If he had the Matthew parable and application he has changed the parable and discarded the judgment application. The wise fisherman is doubtless the Gnostic who *here and now* searches, finds and keeps the "gnosis." Jesus could not have told the story with this meaning. Matthew's version is the more authentic one without question.

Let us turn our attention now to some Synoptic-Thomas parallel parables other than Matthew's great group.

Logion 63 is parallel to Luke's Parable of the Rich Fool (12:16-21). The story is familiar. A rich farmer became even richer by a most abundant crop. With a view only to the material, he planned, he built bigger barns, he stored his goods, he comforted his "soul" in having much goods for many days. On the night he completed all his building and storing, God pronounced doom upon him as a "fool" and he died. The parable closes with a moral: so it is with everyone who lays up treasure for himself, and is not rich toward God.

Thomas' habit is not to *expand* but to condense. It appears then, that Luke has the original form here and Thomas condenses it to suit his purpose as follows:

Logion 63.
Jesus said,
    There was a rich man who had much money. He said, "I will use my money in sowing, reaping, planting, and filling my barns with fruit so I will lack nothing."
    In his heart this was what he thought and that night he died. Whoever has ears let him hear.

This customary warning to "hear" indicates that the Gnostic is to find a "hidden" meaning in this story. The meaning is apparently that *in one's heart* he should consider the *spiritual*, not the material. The judgment sentence from God is not needed since to be in the world is judgment in the mind of the Gnostic. The "whoever has ears" warning replaces the longer Lukan moral.

Logion 64 (Matt. 22:1-14; Luke 14:16-24) is one of the most radically changed of the parallel parables. The change is not one of length but of broad categorical differences. In Matthew this is known as the Parable of the Wedding Feast. Note the differences. To the invitation sent by the host the invited ones responded:

	In Thomas	In Luke
Number one:	Some merchants owed him money. He was to meet them for a setlement that night.	Number one: He had bought a field and he had to go to examine it.
Number two:	He had bought a house and needed that very day to settle it all.	Number two: He had bought five teams of oxen and had to go to check them out.
Number three:	He was arranging for the wedding of a friend; apparently as the "host."	Number three: He had just married and could not leave his bride.
Number four:	He had bought a farm and had to go collect rent.	

Matthew's account gives no dialogue but it does indicate three reactions of those invited: one went to his farm; one went to his business; others seized and mistreated the servants.

In both Thomas and the Synoptics the excuses plainly are just excuses. Luke's excuses have more than a bit of humor in them: One man had bought a farm without seeing it and was now going to see it—*at night!* One had bought ten oxen without testing them and now had to go to see how they worked—*at night!* One had just married and that ended his nights out! Thomas' excuses are more prosaic!

In all three accounts (Matthew, Luke, Thomas) the invitation was then extended to any and all who would come. Those originally invited had, in their rejection, proved themselves unworthy. In Matthew and Luke the house is filled because the host desired it. Thomas ends on a very strongly Gnostic note, i.e., tradesmen and merchants who were held in the very lowest opinion by the Gnostics could not enter the "Father's" house. This last reference to "the places of my Father" is the only thing in Thomas' version which shows understanding that the Synoptic parable related in some way to *God's* invitation to Israel, Israel's rejection, and then God's extending it to all— even those despised by Israel. Thomas' version is closer to Luke than to Matthew. *If* he had Luke, he changed the invitation to make all those originally invited turn out to be unworthy because they were lowly tradesmen and merchants.

The differences in all three are sufficient to warrant the view that all three use separate sources. Dodd[11] and Jeremias[12] have expressed the view that Matthew and Luke have separate sources for this parable, or at least have not depended on a single source. Their works antedate the availability of Thomas. Wilson[13] is very close to this view in saying that Thomas offers "a different version" and that the three may represent a case of "a parable developing in the course of transmission, on its way, in fact, from a Palestinian to a Hellenistic environment." Of the three, Matthew appears to be closer to the original; Luke comes next with a version more colorful and dramatic by means of the dialogue; Thomas appears to be farthest from the original due to his Gnostic coloring. Certainly he did not have Matthew's conclusion (absent in Luke, too) about the guest who was thrown out because he did not have a wedding garment! A good Gnostic could build an entire sermon on the wedding

[11]Dodd, *op. cit.*, p. 121.
[12]Jeremias, *op. cit.*, pp. 37, 53.
[13]Wilson, *op. cit.*, pp. 100-101.

garment as the "gnosis"! Dodd[14] thinks that the "wedding garment" episode was originally a separate parable and that Matthew has used it here to forestall a too-easy acceptance of the Gentiles into the church.

The Parable of the Wicked Husbandmen (Matt. 21:33-46; Mark 12:1-12; Luke 20:9-19; Logion 65) must be considered in this quest for sources. There is unquestionably a parallel in Thomas and the Synoptics. Contextually, its setting is definite and its meaning is clear in the Synoptics. This is not true in Thomas where usually context is not significant. This case may be an exception. Note the details in contrast:

> The Introduction:
> > The details are practically identical except that in Thomas it is a "good" man who prepares and rents the vineyard. This may have no significance except to compare the character of the landlord with that of the workers.
>
> The *Initial* Servants Sent to Collect Rent:
> > Thomas—two servants are sent in succession and both are rejected.
> > Matthew, Mark, Luke—three are sent in succession with the same result.
>
> The *"Many Other"* Servants Sent:
> > Thomas—omits this detail.
> > Luke—omits this detail.
> > Matthew and Mark—include this detail.
>
> The Sending of the Son:
> > All four agree that the son and heir was sent, seized, killed.
> > Mark and Luke add that it was a "beloved" son.
> > Matthew, Mark, and Luke report that the purpose in murdering the son was that the husbandmen might take over the property for themselves.
>
> The Conclusion:
> > Thomas concludes at this point with his usual "Whoever has ears, let him hear."
> > All three Synoptics follow with a long section which applies the story to: Israel's rejection of God's successive messengers and eventually of his Son; God's purpose to trust his kingdom responsibility to other "fruit-bearers," the Gentiles; Jesus' identification of *himself*

---

[14]Dodd, *op. cit.*, p. 122.

with the "rejected stone" motif in Hebrew religious
thought (Ps. 118:22-23; Isa. 8:14-15; 1 Peter 2:4-8);
the desire of Israel's religious leaders to seize and
harm Jesus because they understood that he was
speaking about them.[15]

Thomas, too, follows with the "rejected stone" passage,
but he omits all the other applications and appears
to think of this as a separate saying (Logion 66).

Of the Synoptics, Mark appears to have the original form
and Matthew and Luke appear to have expanded Mark's account. Thomas' intended application seems to be completely
foreign to that of the Synoptics. He has perhaps joined several
logia here for his desired Gnostic purpose. Observe this in
Logia 58-67 as follows.

Logion 58 begins a series of sayings with a definite Gnostic
thrust concerning "finding the Life" (58), looking upon the
"Living One" (59), finding "rest" (60), the one of two who will
"live," and the one who will be filled with "light" (61), Jesus'
mysteries told to those who are "worthy" (62), the "foolish"
rich man (63), the denial of admission to tradesmen and
merchants to "the places" of the "Father" (64), the defaulting
servants under consideration (65), the "rejected stone" (66),
and the tragic lack or loss of the one who "knows the All but
fails to know himself" (67). The presence of the parable in the
midst of a sequence of definite Gnostic concepts indicates that
Thomas understood it to have some "secret" meaning for the
one who had the "gnosis." His presentation could not possibly
be the original intent of a parable told by Jesus. As to *form*,
however, Thomas seems closer to the original. Omit Mark
12:5 and the result is a climactic order: first servant, second
servant, son. This is exactly the order and content in Thomas.

CONCLUSIONS

Thus a review of parabolic sayings and stories parallel in
Thomas and the Synoptics in search of original forms leaves

---

[15]Read Jeremias' discussion, *op. cit.*, p. 57, of the view that Jesus told the
parable, but the church later added an "allegorizing" explanation.

one with some unresolved questions, but with other rather definite conclusions.

1. Where the total saying or parable is concerned, the Synoptics have the form which recommends itself as being the older and the one nearest to Jesus' original saying, perhaps as near as we will ever get, so that in most cases we may feel that we have the *ipsissima verba* of Jesus.

2. There are numerous cases where Thomas has a "color" word or a minor detail which seems likely to be nearer the original than its Synoptic parallels. Examples of this are: the use of "fishermen" rather than the indefinite "they" in the Parable of the Net; the use of "shepherd" rather than "man" in the Parable of the Lost Sheep.

3. Usually the differences in Thomas reflect a definite Gnostic apologetic, thus indicating a time post-dating Jesus.

What are the major values from a study of this work? *First*, perhaps, the reflection of how early in the "pre-canonical" stage of the sayings of Jesus and of the "Gospels" the interpreters started adapting logia from Jesus to their own situation, need, and theological purpose—and how freely they handled these materials.

Second, we gain some insight into Gnosticism in its earliest literary expression. We can weigh some of the views, reflected in the choice of materials, in a larger context than the isolated quotation by admittedly prejudiced "orthodox" interpreters of the Christian faith—Clement, Origen, *et al.* Here is constructive help in understanding those who have been named the "First Systematic Theologians!"

Chapter III

RECENTLY DISCOVERED SAYINGS OF JESUS
(a quest for authenticity)

In the foregoing studies we have examined the Synoptic sayings of Jesus and their parallels in the Gnostic *Gospel According to Thomas* in a quest for sources. Who used whom? Who used what in the respective compositions? We have examined, too, parallel *parabolic sayings* and *parabolic stories* in a quest for original forms. Which account takes us back closer to the fountain whence this stream flows, Jesus of Nazareth?

Now we turn to the most difficult, and perhaps most precarious, quest of all—the question of the *authenticity* of the Thomas sayings attributed to Jesus but not found in the canonical Gospels. Did Jesus say these things? For many scholars this is an unimportant question and the last one which should be asked. They see the importance of the sayings *only* in what they reflect about the life and belief of an apparently Gnostic Christian community of the second century as Christian "theology" was in process of development. That is, of course, the attitude and approach of many scholars to the Synoptic sayings of Jesus. The following discussion assumes that the question of authenticity is in all cases important.

The question of accepting "noncanonical" sayings of Jesus as authentic naturally gives one pause. From the Council of Carthage in A.D. 397 the twenty-seven books commonly called "The New Testament" (but more accurately, perhaps, called "The New Covenant"!) have been regarded as the accepted "Holy Scriptures" of the Christian faith. Many remember, too,

the statement of the Council that *only these and no others*
should be read in the church "under the title of divine Scriptures."[1] With this background the tendency is toward hesitation
at accepting as *authentic sayings of Jesus* anything outside of
the twenty-seven. The temptation is to turn aside for an
excursus into the very interesting question of the authority of
the Council, i.e., "Who *closed* the canon?" That cannot be discussed here.

Estimates of the length of the public ministry of Jesus range
from a few months to a maximum of three and one half years,
depending on the solving of the "feast" problem in John. Under
any condition, the teachings of Jesus included in the Four Gospels appear to represent only a small part of what he said.
Since much more must have been in the floating oral accounts
(which Papias in A.D. 125 still preferred to the *written* accounts!), and since multiple accounts were being written early
(Luke 1:1-4), we do well to examine any saying attributed to
Jesus, particularly in the first two centuries. The Pauline use
of noncanonical sayings of Jesus has already been noted.[2] New
Testament students have found much interest in the Codex
Bezae Luke 6:4 addition.[3]

> When on the same day he saw a man
> working on the Sabbath he said to him,
>   Man, if you know what you are doing,
>   blessed are you.
>   If you know not what you are doing,
>   you are cursed and a transgressor of the Law.

In testing examples of the noncanonical sayings in Thomas
the following categories will be used: The Impossible; The
Possible but not Probable; The Possible and Probable.

---

[1]We do well to recall that this Council also reaffirmed the previous (A.D.
393) canon on the Old Testament and included in it Tobit, Judith, Esdras,
and Maccabees. How long has it been since a sermon was heard on a text from
one of these fascinating but neglected books!
[2]*Supra*, p. 15.
[3]For stimulating treatment of this saying see Joachim Jeremias, *Unknown
Sayings of Jesus* (London: S.P.C.K., 1958), pp. 49-54.

The writer confesses subjectivity but claims honest effort at objectivity in the classification and analysis.

THE IMPOSSIBLE

In this category must be listed the most, by far, of these non-canonical sayings. This is due to the fact that their character is foreign to the character of the canonical sayings and in some instances their spirit is foreign to the spirit of Jesus as reflected in the canonical Gospels and interpreted by his followers. This matter of "foreign character and spirit" is largely bound up with the definite Gnostic apologetic and polemic in the sayings. They were clearly forged as defense measures or as propaganda measures of the Gnostics.[4]

The Gnostic nature of the collection is reflected in the introductory statement that these are "secret" words of the Living Jesus. This is continued in the opening logia.

Logion 1 is a bit discouraging when one tries to interpret some of the very difficult sayings! It states that one must "find the meaning" of these words if he is to avoid "death." Logion 2 continues the idea of "seeking" and closes with the assurance that the one who "finds" will reign over the "All." All this is clearly second-century Gnostic thought. Even Logion 3 which starts out with a "spiritual kingdom" emphasis at least kin to the Synoptics closes with the necessity of "knowing yourselves"; the one who does not "know" himself is in poverty.[5] This idea

---

[4]This apparently is true even though there are many "non-Gnostic" expressions and ideas in some of the sayings, for example:

Logion 6—Gnostic trademark "know" omitted from Matt. 10:10-26.

Logion 25—Social concern reflected is unknown in Gnosticism.

Logion 26—Omits verse 4 from Matt. 7:3-5 where it would strengthen Gnostic idea of "knowledge."

Logion 33—Proclaim from the housetop (Matt. 10:27) does not fit "secret" idea of Gnosticism.

Logion 55—Four persons in same order as Luke 14:26 but omits wife and children. They would be needed in the Gnostic "hate" idea.

Logion 62—Omits "knowledge" idea (Matt. 6:3-4).

Logion 69b—Stresses hunger for *material* things, changing from the *spiritual;* Gnostic would never do this.

[5]Grant and Freedman, *op. cit.*, pp. 120-22, give an excellent discussion of this saying.

of "self-experience" or "self-knowledge" was second-century Gnostic theology.

Logion 4 has been known in part from noncanonical quotation and it has one canonical clause ("for many who are first shall become last") but in its total thrust it is all Gnostic.[6] The saying involves matters of divine revelation if they are such that "an infant of seven days" may instruct an old man about "the place of life." The reference to all "becoming one" is the Gnostic emphasis on the removal of all differences—no "old man of days," "infant of seven days," "last," "first"—all are "one."

Logion 5 continues the Gnostic quest for "gnosis," i.e.—

> Know what is in your sight,
>   and what is concealed will be revealed.
> Because there is nothing hidden which
>   will not be manifest.

This last statement about "nothing hidden which will not be manifest" reflects knowledge of Matthew 10:26 and its Synoptic parallels. The Gnostic force of the Thomas statement in the Coptic text is most apparent when one notes that the Greek text of the Oxyrhynchus version adds "there is nothing buried which shall not be raised up." Since the Coptic appears to be a translation of an older Greek version, it is clear that Thomas has deleted this statement because he understands it to be a reference to resurrection for which the Gnostic had no place in his theology. The saying is at least second century.

Logion 7 is one of the most obscure of the Thomas sayings. One may hope that "avoiding death" does *not* depend on understanding it (Logion 1)!

> Jesus said,
> Blessed is the lion which a man eats
>   that the lion may become a man;
> Cursed is the man whom the lion eats,
>   and the lion becomes a man.

---

[6] Cf. Grant and Freedman, *op. cit.*, p. 84, for review of the Hippolytus citation of a saying *similar* to this in the use of the Naassenes, in parallel with the Coptic and the Oxyrhynchus version of Thomas.

Doresse[7] and Grant[8] think that it is related to the Gnostic idea
of the "world" as a "corpse." "A man eats a lion" (it must be
a corpse before he can eat it) would refer to a man's overcoming the "world," the world is assimilated by the man (the
lion becomes man) and is thus conquered. But if the lion (the
world) eats the man (overcomes him), cursed is the man.[9] One
of the problems involved in the interpretation is that of correct
word order. The reversal of the fourth part of the couplet would
make a perfect *chiasmos*, i.e.—

$$\begin{matrix} \text{Man eats lion} \\ \text{Lion eats man} \end{matrix} \diagup\!\!\!\diagdown \begin{matrix} \text{Lion becomes man} \\ \text{Man becomes lion} \end{matrix}$$

In the first case—"blessed is the man who eats a lion" (overcomes the world). In the second case—"cursed is the man who
is eaten by a lion" (is overcome by the world). This is *not*
Thomas' order; it is *more meaningful* than Thomas' order. Perhaps it requires one who has the "gnosis" to work out that part
of the riddle, too! In any case, this is not a statement from Jesus.

Logion 11 is another of the definitely Gnostic sayings which
join several Gnostic ideas: the passing of everything material;
the removal of all differences; the overcoming of the world. In
part, some of the *ideas* are akin to Synoptic ideas but the
expression is post-Synoptic.

Logia 12 and 13 may be dismissed as coming from Jesus
since they were clearly fabricated to make James and Thomas
the most important of the apostles. James did, indeed, come to
be a leader in the Jerusalem church, but that is all post-Pente-
cost. Thomas came to be glorified by the Gnostics. This adaptation of the Synoptic "Great Confession" is to give this glori-
fication the authority of Jesus. By it Thomas, not Peter, is commended for his discernment and is trusted with the "three
secret words." Reference to previous analysis of this saying
indicates how very Gnostic it is.[10]

---

[7]Doresse, *op. cit.*, p. 371.
[8]Grant and Freedman, *op. cit.*, p. 126.
[9]Gaertner, *op. cit.*, pp. 162-63, has a suggestive development of this idea.
[10]*Supra*, pp. 20-21.

Logion 14 teaches the very opposite of what Jesus taught in Matthew 6:1-18. It reads,

> If you fast, you will beget for yourselves sin;
> If you pray, you will be damned;
> If you give alms, you will do evil to your spirit.

In the Synoptic version Jesus assumes that his disciples, as good Hebrews, will give, pray, and fast, as expressions of their devotion; he tells them how to go about it.

In Logion 14 he says that these practices per se involve sin.[11] This is a Gnostic rejection of the formal and external in divine worship. It is followed by a Thomas emphasis (elsewhere in Matthew) on the nature of true defilement as spiritual.

The "eat what is set before you" embedded in this logion is a Pauline teaching (1 Cor. 10:27). It is, of course, proverbial in nature so Jesus could have used it. Paul does not, however, claim "a word from the Lord" as he likes to do if he has it. Thomas seems to be influenced by the Pauline use.

Logion 15 is not likely a saying of Jesus.

Jesus said,
> When you see him who was not born of woman
> Fall upon your faces and worship him.
> He is your Father.

The first part, "him who was not born of woman," must be a reference to God, the unborn, who is also spoken of as the "Father" of the disciples. He is to be worshipped. Since, however, God cannot be *seen*, the saying must refer to the disciples' coming to recognize Jesus as being "one with" the Father. When they understand his *real* nature they will understand this and worship him as such. This is consistent with other Thomas' sayings which identify him as the "revealer" of

---

[11]Even though in other logia fasting is commended, i.e., Logia 27 and 104. Logion 104 may, however, involve irony rather than instruction, since the one with the "gnosis" would never "come out of the bridal-chamber"; hence, there is no place for fasting!

the Father.[12] It is similar to the Johannine teaching (John 10:30; 14:9) but as it is given here it does not appear to be a genuine saying of Jesus.

Numerous sayings scattered throughout the *Gospel According to Thomas* relate to some definite Gnostic theme and may be conveniently grouped for consideration. There are several such categories.

Little Children—

One theme indicating the nature of the Gnostic has its source in Jesus' Synoptic statement about becoming as little children in order to enter the kingdom (Matt. 18:3). The development in Thomas is, however, completely foreign to that in the Synoptics.

Logion 21.

Mary said to Jesus,
>   Whom are your disciples like?
He said,
>   They are like little children who
>   have taken their place in a field
>   which does not belong to them.
>   When the ones who own the field
>   come they will say, "Let us
>   have our field."
>   They (the children) strip off their
>   clothes before them to release and
>   to return to them (the owners) their field.

Apparently the field is the world (Matt. 13:38) and the children (the Gnostics) do not belong in it. They strip off their clothes, indicating their lack of need of anything of the world. This may even suggest the stripping off of the body in death as they leave the "field" to the grasping ones who do not have the "gnosis" to realize how unimportant the world is.

Logion 22 is on the same theme but expands to the idea of

---

[12]Cf. Logia 5, 17, 59, 61, 62, 108.

the elimination of all differences, all things that would distinguish one from another.

> Jesus saw little children which
> were receiving their mother's milk. He said to
> his disciples,
> > These children who are receiving milk are
> > > like the ones who enter the kingdom.
> They said to him,
> > Shall we, too, being children enter the kingdom?
> Jesus said to them,
> > When you make the two one,
> > When you make the inside as the outside,
> > When you make the top as the bottom,
> > When you make male and female into a single,
> > So the male is not male, and the female not female,
> > When you make eyes an eye,
> > When you make the hand a hand,
> > When you make the foot a foot,
> > An image, an image,
> > Then you will enter.

The saying begins with Jesus' tribute to the childlike nature of those who enter the kingdom. When the disciples ask if they must become children to enter the kingdom, Jesus responds with this very strange answer indicating that entering the kingdom means the elimination of all earthly differences. In Christ there is no male and female, top and bottom, inside and outside. Everything must be understood in its true nature. Only the *real* is important.

Numerous passages have been cited in the New Testament to indicate the idea of *unity* in the kingdom. The one which seems most apt is a statement, not from Jesus but from Paul, i.e., Galatians 3:28, "There is neither Jew nor Greek, slave nor freeman, male nor female; for you are all one in Christ Jesus." In Gnostic thought the eternal state will be like what they understood the primal state to be. In it they held that primal man was androgynous. The true Gnostic rejected sex as a part of the evil world which must be to him as a corpse. He gives up a physical eye or hand (symbol of evil in Matthew 5:29, 30) and receives instead a "spiritual eye" or "spiritual hand."

This idea of "oneness" is continued in Logion 23 where Jesus says he will choose "two out of ten thousand" and the two will be as one.

Logion 37 continues the idea of stripping off one's clothes, i.e., of denying the world, renouncing the material, experiencing self-understanding.

> His disciples said,
>> When will you be manifest to us,
>>> When will we see you?
> Jesus said,
>> When you strip off your clothes without shame
>> And take your clothes and trample them
>>> under your feet as little children
>> Then (you will see?) the Son of
>>> the Living
>> And you will not fear.

Such renunciation and self-understanding experience is essential for seeing him in his manifestation.

Logion 46 states that one who becomes a child shall "know the kingdom" and shall become "higher" than John the Baptist who was the "highest" of those born of women. This, of course, is very close to a Synoptic pronouncement, but the matter of becoming a child has been added.

Logion 106 states that "when you make the two one," that is, eliminate all differences, "you will become sons of man." Such ones will be able to move mountains, that is, the world will have no power over them. They will be free of its domination.

The climax of the expression of this necessary elimination of all differences is found in the very last and strangest statement.

> Logion 114.
>
> Simon Peter said to them,
>> Let Mary depart from us because
>>> women are not worthy of The Life.
> Jesus said,
>> Behold (Look), I will lead her
>>> so that I will change her
>>> to male, in order that

> she also may become a
> living spirit like you males.
> For every female who
> makes herself male will enter
> the kingdom of heaven.

On the surface this is one of the logia one hopes Jesus did *not* say! Actually, it carries forward in a very dramatic way the idea of the obliteration of distinctions in the realm of the kingdom. Mary here is no doubt Mary Magdalene. In other Gnostic writings the idea of trouble between her and Simon Peter is reflected! Here Simon (the group "spokesman" of the Synoptics but not in Thomas) suggests that the followers of Jesus ban Mary from their company because females have no part in the Life of "gnosis." This reflects again the low esteem in which the Gnostics held women.

Jesus, however, proposes a work of new creation on her part. He will change her so she will no longer be female but male. Then she will be able to enter the kingdom. All differences between her and the other followers in the group will have been removed. It is good Gnostic teaching but completely foreign to the spirit of Jesus and of the New Testament teachings. The only thing like it would be the Pauline statement quoted above, or Jesus' statement that in the resurrection there will be neither marrying nor giving in marriage (Matt. 22:30). This, of course, is not because the female will be changed to male, but because it will be life on a different plane which transcends human relationships and functions.

The World as a Corpse—

This is another thematic category in the Thomas sayings. It appears in multiple variations, but always there is the basic idea that the material, evil world is "dead" as far as the true Gnostic is concerned.

Logion 56.

Jesus said,
> The one who has understood the world
> has discovered a corpse,

> And whoever has discovered a corpse,
>   of him the world is unworthy.

Really to understand the true nature of the cosmic order is to understand that it is "dead" as far as the true "life" is concerned. This "dead" world is not worthy of the occupancy of the one who has the "gnosis." He will leave it behind.

Logion 60 involves this idea in a testing of wits type of object lesson sometimes found in the Gospels. Jesus and his disciples saw a Samaritan carrying a lamb on his way to Judea.

> Jesus asked,
>   [Why] is this man [carrying] the lamb?
> They answer,
>   In order that he may kill and eat it.
> He said,
>   While it lives he will not eat it;
>   [He will eat it] only if he kills it and
>   it becomes a corpse.

They agree that the lamb is not in danger of being eaten unless it becomes a corpse. Jesus then says,

> *You,* seek for yourself a place of rest,
>   so you may not become a corpse
>   and be eaten.

These are, indeed, words with "secret" (hidden) meanings! There may be some significance in a *Samaritan* on his way to *Judea* with a *lamb*—some "Passover" or other religious significance. This is not developed. The meaning seems to be in the need for Jesus' disciples to seek a "place" of "rest" lest they become a corpse like the world and be destroyed. Both "place" (*topos*) and "rest" (*anapausis*) are Gnostic words of superior importance. The warning would be, "Seek until you find the 'gnosis' lest you be overcome by the corpse-like world."

Logion 80 is almost a restatement of Logion 56. The only difference is that Logion 56 has "corpse" (*ptoma*) and Logion 80 has "body" (*soma*). The difference may be coincidental due to the similarity of the Greek words standing behind the Cop-

tic. If the two logia were connected in Thomas it would suggest
that the physical body (*soma*) as understood by the Gnostic
was in reality a corpse (*ptoma*). In both logia the world is not
worthy of the one who makes the discovery that the world is a
"corpse" or a "body." Similar to this is the Logion 111 statement
that the world is not worthy of "whoever finds himself." To
discover the true "corpse-like" nature of the world appears to
be to find oneself. Too, the one who "finds the world" is to
"deny" the world (Logion 110).

Logion 112 is on a similar theme.

Jesus said,
        Woe to the flesh which depends upon the soul.
        Woe to the soul which depends upon the flesh.

Rhetorically this is another instance of *chiasmos*.

$$\begin{matrix} \text{Flesh} & \diagdown\!\!\!\!\diagup & \text{Soul} \\ \text{Soul} & \diagup\!\!\!\!\diagdown & \text{Flesh} \end{matrix}$$

It is likely a Gnostic proverb and well known. Flesh (*sarx*) and
soul (*psuche*) were antithetical in Gnostic thought as in Greek
thought. Either depending on the other would be wretched.
This same idea is in Logion 29.

        If the flesh (*sarx*) has come to be because of the spirit
            (*pneuma*) it is a marvel.
        If the spirit (*pneuma*) has come to be because of the body
            (*soma*) it is a marvel of marvels.
        But I marvel at how this treasure has
            made its home in poverty.

The "treasure" is the spirit; the "poverty" in which it has made
its home is the "body" or the "flesh." The two words seem to
mean the same thing here.

Logion 87 is a third variation of this same saying.

        Wretched is the body (*soma*) which depends on a body;
        Wretched is the soul (*psuche*) which depends on the two.

One must learn not to depend upon anything of the world. It
is wretched for one to feel that he needs the body. It is more

wretched for him to feel that it is necessary for body and soul to hold together in order to experience true "being." The soul must not depend upon the world. Those who do not see this are "drunk" and "blind" (Logion 28).

The Solitaries—

One who had the "gnosis" was spoken of as a "solitary." These stand over against all others, even members of their own families.

Logion 16 begins with a "Synoptic-like" statement that men are deceived in thinking that he has come to cover the world with peace, he has come rather to cover it with divisions—fire, sword, war. His presence calls people to "take sides" thus bringing about division. Then come the words,

> There shall be five in a house.
> Three shall be against two,
> Two shall be against three,
> The father against the son,
> The son against the father.
> They will stand as solitaries.

To receive the "gnosis" and stand for Jesus is to be isolated from the world. Again, the rhetoric reveals a studied literary form.

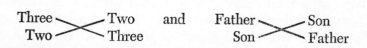

This is a piece of Gnostic propaganda.

Logion 49 pronounces a blessing upon the "solitary" ones. In this logion Jesus identifies them as the "elect," the chosen ones. He says they will find the kingdom because they have come from it and they will go to it again. Because they are the solitary, the elect, the enlightened, their source is the kingdom and their destiny is the kingdom. It is their "whence" and their "whither."

In the following logion (50) Jesus instructs his disciples that if anyone asks whence they come, they are to answer that they "have come from the Light, where the Light began of itself." If anyone asks who they are, they are to answer that they "are the elect ones of the Living Father." They are "solitaries." If anyone asks what is in them which is a sign of the Father's presence, they are to answer that the sign is "a movement and a rest," a "movement" which comes to a "rest," a good Gnostic word and idea. They have reached the "gnosis."

Logia 74 and 75 appear to be separate sayings which Thomas has brought into juxtaposition to form a sort of dialogue.

Logion 74.

He said,
> Lord, many are standing around the well [or spring]
> but no one is in the well [or spring].

Logion 75.

Jesus said,
> Many are standing at the door,
> but the solitary are the ones
> who will go into the bridal chamber.

The "well" is no doubt the spiritual water which comes from the mouth of Jesus. In Logion 12 Jesus said that he was no longer on a master-servant relationship with Thomas because Thomas had drunk from that stream. In Logion 108 Jesus says that the one who drinks from that stream will become identified with him and will receive the revelation of the "secret things." Logion 74, then, appears to indicate that many are near the stream but are not taking advantage of it.

Jesus' response, Logion 75, is that many stand at the door of the festive bridal chamber but only the "solitaries" go in. These are the enlightened ones. The suggestion may come from the Synoptic Parable of the Ten Virgins. The juxtaposition of the two separate logia cleverly puts Jesus into the position of identifying the "solitary ones" as those who drink from the stream which flows from his mouth.

Judaism Rejected—

Two other logia in juxtaposition round out this sampling of "sayings" which could hardly come from Jesus. Both of these relate to a rejection of basic Judaism.

Logion 52.

His disciples said to him,
    Twenty-four prophets spoke in Israel;
        they all spoke of you.
He said to them,
    You have dismissed the Living
        who is with you and have
        spoken of those who are dead.

The "twenty-four" doubtless is a reference to the twenty-four books of the Hebrew Scriptures which were read in their synagogues. The disciples' statement reflects the view that these books spoke of Jesus—an idea well known in the canonical Gospels (Luke 24:25-27; John 5:39), but there it is always Jesus, not the disciples, calling attention to the fact.

Jesus' reaction is one of near impatience that the disciples should be going back to the Hebrew prophets for confirmation of his person. The prophets were dead; Jesus was here in living presence with them.

Logion 53 is a definite rejection of the most basic ritual of Judaism, circumcision.

His disciples said to him,
    Is circumcision profitable or not?
He said to them,
    If it were profitable, their (infants')
        father would beget them
        circumcized from their mother.
    The true circumcision in spirit
        is profitable in every way.

There is nothing in the canonical Gospels which gives any impression that Jesus rejected the covenant ritual of his people.

In John 7:22-23 he even points out with seeming approval that the law of circumcision supersedes the law of the Sabbath. This logion surely did not come from Jesus.

What was its likely origin? Not Thomas (the collector) who does not argue from the viewpoint of what is "profitable" because it is "natural." He does, however, add this to his collection of formal religious practices rejected: praying, fasting, giving alms, observing dietary laws, circumcision.

The logion is doubtless a product of the influence of Paul. One can almost hear Paul saying, "I wish I had said that!" He did not. If he had had the saying as "a word from the Lord" the ecumenical council in Acts 15 would have ended much earlier! The Judaizers would have been put to speedy rout.

The idea *is* Pauline. In Romans 2:29, 1 Corinthians 7:18-19, Galatians 6:15, Colossians 2:11, Philippians 3:3, he argues that what is important is not what is "physical"—Jew, Gentile—but what is "spiritual"—a "new creature," a new creation in Christ. What the covenant ritual of circumcision stood for, a meaningful relationship of faith commitment to God, is a spiritual matter. It was a memorial to right relationship to God; hence, the true "circumcision" is a spiritual one. It was an argument to delight Gentile Christians—and Gnostics!

THE POSSIBLE BUT NOT PROBABLE

There is in Thomas a small number of noncanonical sayings attributed to Jesus which Jesus may possibly have said. The probability is that he did not. These are sayings which are not foreign to the spirit of his teachings and which, in some instances, bear remarkable likeness to his method. The decision of authenticity is largely a subjective decision.

In the last category Logion 14 was cited as foreign to the spirit of Jesus since it was an outright rejection of fasting, praying, and giving alms, whereas, in Matthew 6:1-18 Jesus appears to assume these practices and to endorse them *when properly practiced* as genuine devotion rather than play acting.

Logion 6 is much closer to this.

His disciples asked him,
> Do you wish us to fast?
> How should we pray?
> How should we give alms?
> What diet should we keep?

Jesus said,
> Do not lie.
> Do not what you hate.
> Because all things are manifest
> in the sight of heaven.

One can imagine the situation which gave rise to the disciples' question: such a scene as that in which the Pharisees complained that Jesus and his disciples did not observe all the religious laws (Mark 2:18, a complaint about fasting; Matt. 9:11, a complaint about eating; Matt. 12:1-2, a complaint about the Sabbath observance). The disciples ask Jesus as to his wishes about these matters. Jesus' answer indicates that what is important is the true inner matters such as honesty ("Do not lie") and fair treatment ("Do not what you hate"). "Heaven" sees all things, the internal as well as the external, and the internal is what is important.

In Matthew 7:12 Jesus gives a *positive* framework to the famous Tobit-Hillel dictum about doing to no one that which one hates. The Thomas statement is closer to the original *negative* form. The religious fiction book Tobit, a second-century B.C. work, was a favorite of the Hebrew people because it reflected the conduct of the good Hebrew. When Tobit[13] was sending his son Tobias on the journey to bring back the treasure he had left on deposit, he gave Tobias some good advice including

What you hate, do to no one (Tobit 4:15).

Years later there was a story circulated among the Jews that a heathen challenged the great teacher of Israel, Hillel,[14] by saying,

---

[13]*The Apocrypha*, Revised Standard Version (New York: Thomas Nelson and Sons, 1957), p. 57.

[14]N. N. Glatzer, *The Rest is Commentary* (Boston: Beacon Press, 1961), p. vii.

> Convert me by teaching me the entire Torah (Law)
> while I stand here on one foot.

Hillel answered (quoting Tobit),

> What you hate, do to no one.
> That is the law and the prophets, everything else is commentary.
> Go and learn what that means.

In Thomas Jesus says,

> Do not what you hate.

In Matthew Jesus says,

> Whatever you wish others to do for you, do so for them.
> This is the law and the prophets.

Actually, he *could* have said both!

Logion 98 has been cited by some scholars as a saying which may have come from Jesus. In Luke 14:31 Jesus uses an illustration about a king who proposes war with another king. He plans very carefully how he will conduct the battle because the odds are against him two to one. The enemy king has twenty thousand soldiers; he has only ten thousand. Jesus used it in a setting on "counting the cost" of becoming one of Jesus' disciples and being in a minority where the opposition is appalling.

Thomas' logion is similar.

> Jesus said,
> The kingdom of the Father is like a man who wants to
> kill a strong man.
> He drew his sword while in his house, and thrust it into
> the wall in order to know if his hand would push it
> through.
> Then he killed the strong man.

Two matters make it improbable that Jesus said this. The "kingdom of the Father" is a Thomas trademark; "kingdom of heaven" or "of God" is the Synoptic pattern though Jesus does refer to the righteous as "shining forth in the kingdom of their Father" (Matt. 13:43).

Again, the Thomas story seems to glorify murder, personal hostility. This was completely foreign to Jesus' teaching. He did recognize the inevitability of wars and did not hesitate to use such an illustration as that of the king. It is less likely that he would use the "murder" illustration.

Jesus could have said Logion 105 if some interpreters are right in thinking that it should be punctuated as a question.

> Jesus said,
>> Whoever knows father and mother shall be called the son
>> of a harlot.

It is very difficult to get even a Gnostic meaning out of this saying as it stands. Grant[15] punctuates it as a declarative statement and relates it to John 8:42 where the "Jews" imply that *Jesus (not they)* was born of fornication. They did not know who his father was. Jesus knew (John 8:55) that God was his Father. Grant wonders if Thomas has this in mind and adds the "mother" idea with a reference to the Holy Spirit. In some Gnostic writings[16] the Holy Spirit (Wisdom) was the mother of Jesus. This is very difficult to follow.

Doresse[17] does not discuss the saying at all but he does punctuate it as a question,

> He who knows father and mother, shall he be called "son of a
> harlot"?

If this is correct, the saying would fit perfectly into the John 8 controversy. *He* knew his Father and his mother. Should he then be called by such insulting name? It is quite clear that if Jesus *did* say it, the Johannine tradition did not have it. It fits too well to have been omitted.

THE POSSIBLE AND PROBABLE

This is the most subjective of the three categories proposed

---

[15]Grant and Freedman, *op. cit.*, pp. 191-92.
[16]*Pistis Sophia.*
[17]Doresse, *op. cit.*, p. 369.

for this analysis. Which noncanonical sayings in Thomas recommend themselves as the ones most probably *authentic* sayings of Jesus? We may do well to take a canonical text in paraphrase, "Let him who is without his favorite theory cast the first stone." I recommend five for your consideration. They are presented in the "order of probability" from least to greatest.

Logion 102.

Jesus said,
> Woe to the Pharisees.
> They are like a dog sleeping in the manger of the oxen.
> He does not eat.
> Nor does he permit the oxen to eat.

This is like Jesus' warnings against the religious leaders of the Jews in the Synoptics. In Luke 11:52-53 Jesus complained that the scribes (of the Pharisaic party?) had the keys but would neither enter nor permit others to enter. Thomas used that in another logion (30).

In Logion 102 the charge is even more dramatic. Some have felt that Jesus would not have likened the Pharisees to a dog. Why not? He likened them to whitewashed graves. He likened Herod to a fox!

The dog in the manger is, of course, a proverb. It is a very old proverb. Today it is usually listed in the fables of Aesop, who, according to Herodotus, lived in Greece in 550 B.C. The fable, like most of the others, has never been traced back that far. It appears in multiple variations. In some the dog will not permit horses to eat; in others the dog will not permit oxen to eat. In some the animals address their unhappiness to the dog; in some they address their unhappiness to one another; in some there is simply an "aside" remark on how *like people* the dog is! Some variations are long; some are short. This is the simplest version:

> A dog, seeking a cool place for an afternoon nap, stole into the manger of an ox. He lay there on the soft straw and soon fell asleep. Soon the ox, returning from an afternoon's work in the field, entered his barn intending to eat some of the straw. As

the dog awoke, snarling and growling to keep the ox from his
food, the ox with forbearance remarked, "What a miserable
animal. He will not eat nor will he allow others to eat."

The fable has been traced back to the middle of the second
century A.D. in works other than Thomas. Lucian of Samosata,
who was born A.D. 125, uses it twice. In his *Timon the Misan-
thrope,* when Zeus is talking to Plutus about people whose only
enjoyment is to keep others from enjoying the friendship of
Plutus he calls them "true dogs in the manger."[18] There is a
second and more definitive reference in his devastating satirical
essay, *To an Illiterate Book-Fancier.* He chides the collector for
buying rare books, locking them up, neither reading them nor
permitting anyone else to do so! He charges him, "True to your
dog-in-the-manger principles, you neither eat the corn yourself, nor give the horse a chance."[19]

In this same essay, in chiding the Book-Fancier about his
inability to change, Lucian asks the question, "Shall the Ethi-
opian change his skin?" This, too, is an old proverb. Jeremiah
had used it eight hundred years before Lucian did (Jer. 13:23).
This reflects Lucian's acquaintance with wisdom materials at
least known in Hebrew religious circles.

It can be charged that, since the dog in the manger is a
proverb, Thomas could have picked it up from common use.
This is very true. So could Jesus; and it is very much like his
teachings elsewhere recorded.

Logion 47 adds two more proverbs to the many attributed to
Jesus both in and out of the canonical Gospels.

Jesus said,
> It is impossible for a man to ride two horses and to stretch
> two bows.

The second part of the logion is from the Synoptics, "it is impossible for a servant to serve two masters."

---

[18]H. W. and F. G. Fowler (trans.), *The Works of Lucian of Samosata* (Oxford: The Clarendon Press, 1949), I, 36.
[19]*Ibid.,* III, 278.

This is wisdom literature. Serving two masters is like riding two horses in different directions! It is like shooting at two targets in different places! It is impossible and frustrating and destructive to human personality. The saying lends itself to credence as a genuine saying of Jesus.

Logion 97 presents one of the most suggestive of the new parables attributed to Jesus.

> Jesus said,
>> The kingdom of the Father is like a woman carrying a jar full of meal.
>> While she was walking on a long road, the handle of the jar broke.
>> The meal spilled out behind her on the road.
>> She did not know, she had noticed no trouble.
>> When she entered her house, she put the jar down.
>> She found it empty.

The saying has all the characteristics of a genuine parable from Jesus. It is a perfect warning of the danger of letting the good things of the kingdom slip away when they are right in one's grasp. It is like the many who were about the well, but with no one drawing water from it (Logion 74).

Logion 43 presents a comparison which bears the marks of an authentic saying of Jesus. Jesus rebukes his disciples for lack of discernment in not being able to detect his *identity* by means of his *teachings*. He says they are

>> like the Jews who
>> love the tree but hate the fruit
>> or love the fruit but hate the tree.

The rhetorical pattern of *chiasmos* suggests a proverbial nature of the saying.

As such it may well be an authentic saying in which Jesus chides his disciples for being slow to make up their minds. It is similar to the Synoptic (Matt. 11:16-17) rebuke of the people who could not make up their minds. Jesus said they were like children who could not decide whether to play wedding and be happy, or play funeral and be sad! Logion 43 presents the same incisive teaching with a different analogy.

Logion 82 is the saying most likely to be accepted by any person inclined to accept any of the sayings as genuine.[20]

> Jesus said,
> > Whoever is near me is near the fire.
> > Whoever is far from me is far from the kingdom.

Elsewhere in Thomas Jesus speaks of setting a fire upon the earth (Logia 10, 16). In the Synoptics his coming meant the presence of the testing fire of God's presence (Luke 12:49). Jesus told a Jewish teacher of the law who agreed with him on the essence of genuine relationship to God, "You are not far from the kingdom" (Mark 12:34). The presence of Jesus in the world meant that God's kingdom, his rule, had broken into history. Like a purging fire it would sweep the world. To be near Jesus meant to be near that fire. To be far from him meant to be far from the kingdom and God. This was the teaching of Jesus whether recorded in Synoptics, in Thomas, or never recorded at all.

---

[20]Origen, *supra*, p. 16, knew this as a saying of Jesus. Wilson, *Studies in the Gospel of Thomas*, p. 111, cites a work unavailable for this research (J. B. Bauer, "Echte Jesusworte?" in *Evangelium aus dem Nilsand*, [Frankfurt am Main, 1960]) as inclined to the view that this is an authentic saying. Joachim Jeremias, *Unknown Sayings of Jesus*, p. 55, states that "there can be no doubt that this has the ring of a genuine saying of Jesus."

Chapter IV

THE THEOLOGICAL STANCE OF
THE GOSPEL ACCORDING TO THOMAS

The intriguing philosophy of existentialism which has captured the minds of twentieth-century man has given to the world the most expressive term, "being and becoming." I *am*, but I am also *becoming*. I am never static. I *am* a person but I am *becoming* more of the person that I am, which may turn out to be an entirely different person.

When the Thomas sayings were collected sometime in the second century, Christian "theology" was in the "becoming" category. Earlier we have noted that the Gnostics have been called the first systematic theologians. The Christian leaders, writers—in fact, the total Christian community—were producing a theology. They were hammering it out as metal workers, carving it out as sculptors, molding it out as potters. To borrow Jeremiah's beautiful object lesson of the potter and the clay (Jer. 18:1-6), sometimes their product turned out to be a "marred vessel" (AV) or a "spoiled vessel" (RSV) and had to be remolded. Sometimes the product proved to be so very bad that it had to be discarded completely and the work had to be done all over. The Christian community, testing itself against itself, testing itself by what "Scriptures" it had, checking itself as man in community, and always seeking the way of the Spirit, proved to be equal to the task.

The theology of Thomas is Gnostic theology, a theology which ultimately, in its full-grown form, was rejected by the main stream of Christian thought. But the theology of Thomas is the mildest extant expression of Gnosticism. It is Gnosticism before it faded away into the wild fancies of unchained imagination in the later centuries.

Wilson[1] is correct in insisting that "Gnosticism is not simply a depraved form of Christianity." It has deep roots in the Hellenistic world. It weaves into Christianity threads of Greek philosophy uniting the Christian concept of redemption with the Greek concept of deliverance from the world and its controlling "powers."

Doresse[2] raises the question, "Is the *Gospel of Thomas* orthodox?" In the Socratic style of changing a question into a question, we may counter, "Orthodox by what standard of measurement?" By measurement of the main stream of Christian thinkers of the second and third centuries (Irenaeus, Clement, Origen, Tertullian)? No, though they were not entirely free of its influence. By measurement of the Scriptures which came to be accepted by Christian consensus by the Council of Carthage in A.D. 397? No, though even in their rejection of incipient Gnosticism, Paul, John, and the writer of the *Epistle to the Hebrews* show traces of common ground, or at least dip into the common dish of theological terminology. By measurement of the orthodoxy represented in the great Christian "confessional" statements (from the *Apostles' Creed* to the latest in 1967)? No. By measurement of the "orthodoxy" of Christian faith of the twentieth century? No, though that is very difficult to define. *I* am the only really "orthodox" person I know! Aren't you? Dr. H. E. Dana frequently chided and challenged his students with the statement, "Orthodoxy is my-doxy and heterodoxy is your-doxy!"[3] The following analysis is no effort to "baptize" Gnosticism! It is an attempt at an honest look at Gnosticism in this earliest extant form.

Look at the theology reflected in the *Gospel of Thomas* as a theology in evolution. It is a phase of Christianity on its way, Christian thought moving out of a Hebrew cradle into a Hel-

---

[1]Wilson, *The Gnostic Problem*, p. 106.
[2]Doresse, *op. cit.*, pp. 348-52.
[3]Professor of New Testament at Southwestern Baptist Theological Seminary, 1919-1938.

lenistic world. As it is in natural evolution, some forms did not survive the changing "climates" of the centuries. They burned out under the white heat of the light which coming into the world lighteth every man, the light which cannot be suppressed by whatever "darkness," the light which keeps on shining (John 1:1-9).

THE FATHER

The too-neglected but all-important study of *comparative religion* reveals that the nature of a religion is determined by the nature of its concept of God. Man comes to be like that which he worships. "Worship" comes to us from the old English "worthship." What has "worth" takes first place in man's thought. What takes first place in man's thought determines what the man comes to be like; hence, "like God"—"like man."

In later Gnostic thought the god with which man and the world had most to do was the god of creation. In Gnostic thought he was a corrupt god. In another of the Nag Hammadi books, *The Apocryphon of John,* his name is Ialdabaoth. He is the son of Sophia, the twelfth and lowest of the "aeons." Her own instability caused her to fall from the world of light into outer darkness. Without letting her mate know what she was doing she spontaneously and of her power alone conceived and produced this son. He was a stupid son. He created the world and later engaged in a struggle with Christ to prevent Christ from giving the "gnosis" to Adam and Eve. He failed and Christ led Adam and Eve into the "light." Grant[4] wonders if the name Ialdabaoth is not a corruption of the three Hebrew names for God, Yahweh, Elohe, Sabaoth.

There is nothing of this in the *Gospel of Thomas.* Here God is practically identified with Jesus, the Son. This may be an extension of the Johannine idea of the "oneness" of Father and Son.

---

[4]R. M. Grant, "Gnosticism," *The Interpreter's Dictionary of the Bible* (New York: Abingdon Press, 1962), II, 405.

This identification has been observed earlier[5] in Logion 15.

> When you see him who was not born of woman
> Fall upon your faces and worship him.
> He is your Father.

To repeat, the first part, "him who was not born of woman," must be a reference to God, *the unborn*. Since, however, God is also *the unseen*, the reference must be to the Son also. When the disciples recognize Jesus' *true nature* they will recognize his "oneness" with the Father. Such a God as Jesus reveals, even in Thomas, has nothing in common with the ultimate Gnostic concept of God.

Logion 50 presents another expression of this identification of Jesus the Son ("The Light") and God the Father ("The Living Father").

> Jesus said,
>   If they ask you, "What is your origin?"
>   Answer them, "Our origin is the Light, where the Light of
>   itself came to be. . . ."
>   If they ask you, "Who are you?"
>   Answer, "We are his sons and the chosen of the Living
>   Father. . . ."

In the second expression, "his" (in "his sons") appears to have the "Light" as its antecedent. Jesus is the "Light." This is followed by the statement of their belonging to the Living Father, God. There is virtual identity.

The most frequently used expression of God is the term, "Father," a good canonical Gospel term. Over and over the kingdom is presented as "the kingdom of the Father." This is true in many of the "kingdom" parables where the Synoptic parallels have "kingdom of God" or "kingdom of heaven." As the true Gnostic would not pronounce the unutterable Gnostic name of Jesus (Logion 13), so Thomas is reluctant to use the unutterable name of God. Only in the Synoptic saying "Give to God God's things" (Logion 100) is the word used by

---

[5]*Supra*, p. 58.

Thomas as a reference to the deity. Elsewhere it is the "Father" (Logia 3, 27, 40, 44, 50, 57, 61, 64, 69, 76, 83, 96, 97[?], 98, 99, 113).

THE HOLY SPIRIT

The *Gospel of Thomas* has only one reference to the Holy Spirit. It is identical with the Synoptic saying regarding blasphemy.

Logion 44.

Jesus said,
    Whoever blasphemes the Father,
      it shall be forgiven him.
    Whoever blasphemes the Son,
      it shall be forgiven him.
    Whoever blasphemes the Holy Spirit,
      it shall not be forgiven him either on earth or in heaven.

This is the second in a chain of logia which Thomas may have grouped for a theological purpose (43, 44, 45, 46, 47). Logion 43 reflects Jesus rebuking his disciples because they cannot detect his *identity* in his *teachings*. He tells them they are

    like the Jews who
    love the tree but hate the fruit
    or love the fruit but hate the tree.

The rhetorical pattern of *chiasmos*,

    Love the tree ╲╱ Hate the fruit
    Love the fruit ╱╲ Hate the tree

indicates a proverbial saying which, by repeated use, has come to be a set form. It may well be an authentic saying of Jesus in rebuking his disciples for failure to make proper distinctions. This is similar to his Synoptic rebuke of the people who could not make up their minds about what they wanted (Matt. 11:

16-17); they were like children arguing over whether to play "wedding" and make merry music or to play "funeral" and make sad music. In the Synoptics this is in a "John the Baptist" setting; in Thomas the same "John the Baptist" setting follows closely in Logion 46.

In the chain, Logion 45 is the Synoptic saying about fruit trees and their respective fruits. Logion 46 is the Synoptic saying about making proper distinctions and recognizing the true nature of John and of Jesus. Logion 47 interweaves the Synoptic sayings about serving two masters, putting new wine into old wineskins, patching a garment, and a new saying about the impossibility of riding two horses in opposite directions or shooting two arrows at different targets.

Embedded in this chain of logia relating to "true nature" and "proper distinctions" is Logion 44 on the sin of blaspheming the Holy Spirit. *By its very nature* it is a sin for which there is no forgiveness. This is exactly the meaning of the Synoptic passage.

THE SON

While the doctrine of deity in the *Gospel of Thomas* may be safely called "Trinitarian" (Logion 44), the divine person most clearly and frequently presented is the Son.

In many of the logia the reference to the Son is a reference to the *"historical Jesus."*[6] In Logion 31 Jesus is the prophet without honor in his own village, the physician who will not be called by those who know him. In Logion 38 he is the one who will one day be sought but not found by men (probably a reference to his death). In Logion 61 he reclines at the table with Salome and speaks to her of his having come from the Father to reveal light to those in darkness. In Logion 72 he is so human that he is asked to be an arbiter between brothers

---

[6]After completing the research for this study I noted that, at the meeting of the Society for New Testament Studies in Austria in August, 1966, Helmut Koester read a paper on "The Historical Jesus in Second Century Gospels." I hope to see the article in print soon.

who are quarreling over the division of an inheritance. In Logion 78 he appears to be the man unbent by the winds and living the rugged life of the open, a reference which, in the Synoptics, is applied to John the Baptist.

In Logion 79 a woman from the crowd praises the mother who bore and nursed the infant who is now the man, Jesus. In Logion 86 he is the homeless one when night comes, is less privileged than the foxes which have dens and the birds which have roosting places. In Logion 99 this man Jesus is sought by his anxious mother and brothers. In Logion 100 he is asked to settle the mundane question of paying taxes. In Logion 101 this human Jesus was by his earthly mother born to death but by his heavenly mother[7] born to life. In Logion 104 he is so human that he must face the question of fasting. And in Logion 105 he is so human that enemies not knowing the identity of his father call him "son of harlot."

This emphasis on the human Jesus does not, however, embrace the total of his person in the *Gospel of Thomas*. There are sayings which relate to his *redemptive death*. Doresse[8] sees a veiled reference to his death as a sacrificial lamb in Logion 60. This is the saying discussed earlier in which Jesus carries on a test of wits with his disciples over the Samaritan who is carrying a lamb up to Judea where he will kill it and eat it. Doresse's interpretation is not convincing. As indicated earlier, this saying belongs in the cycle of sayings depicting the world as a corpse. It is a warning to the disciples that they not become "corpse-like" and be destroyed. Montefiore[9] sees the lamb as a symbol of the Gnostic in danger of being devoured by a hostile world—the Samaritan. Gaertner,[10] on the other hand, thinks the Samaritan represents the evil god, the Demiurge, who is determined to kill the lamb, the Gnostic, by keeping him enslaved by the material world.

Logion 65, like its parallel in the Synoptics (the Parable of

[7]Wisdom, in other Gnostic works.
[8]Doresse, *op. cit.*, p. 344.
[9]Montefiore, *op. cit.*, pp. 93-94.
[10]Gaertner, *op. cit.*, pp. 166-69.

the Wicked Husbandmen), does appear to refer to the death of Jesus as the Son of God and the last messenger of God to a disobedient Israel. His rejection marks the point of God's giving the stewardship of his "vineyard" to others, the Gentiles.

Logion 66 continues this idea as it is continued in the Synoptics with the "rejected stone" passage. Jesus, rejected by those who were supposed to be building God's "house," proves to be the one most essential stone in the structure.[11]

Jesus is depicted as the *risen Christ* in the *Gospel of Thomas*. In the very first sentence of the Gospel he is introduced as "the Living Jesus." As the Living Jesus he is the *author* of the "sayings" and the *revealer* of the "gnosis." The sayings are of such importance that to find their hidden meaning means "life" and to fail to find it means "death" (Logion 1). Doresse[12] questions whether or not as the *revealer* he is the "child of seven days" who in Logion 4 imparts instruction to an old man. This seems to be highly unlikely. The saying refers only to the very nature of the "gnosis" as a matter of divine revelation versus human understanding if a child can teach it to the aged.

His being the risen or Living Christ seems to be the force of Logion 37 in which the disciples ask when they will see him, when he will be revealed to them. In his answer Jesus tells them under what conditions they will see him and refers to it as their seeing the "Son of the Living." This may mean the "Son of the Living One," i.e., the Father; or it may be a descriptive, "the Living Son." In either view the reference makes no sense apart from a "seeing" which is other than seeing the historical Jesus who is speaking to them.

Jesus in the *Gospel of Thomas* is the mystical one who is *outside of the world* so the disciples must ask him in Logion 24 to show them the "place" where he is, a Gnostic concept. Jesus answers with mysterious words about his being a "light" within men to dispel their darkness.

---

[11]These are all the possible references to Jesus' death. The paucity compared with the many references to his "human" life may denote an incipient docetism which was fully developed in later Gnostic thought.

[12]Doresse, *op. cit.*, p. 344.

He is at the same time one who is *present in the world.* In Logion 28 he speaks of having come to stand in the world and to examine men. He found them "drunk" (in Gnostic thought this means ignorant of salvation), and not one of them "thirsting for water." So his soul suffered for men who were so "blind" that they could not see that the world is a temporary place. Man comes into it "empty"; he leaves it "empty." He longs for the time when men will throw off their "drunkenness" (the first step toward salvation) and turn to another frame of mind; perhaps he means turn to "thirsting" for the water he offers.

There is one very strange saying concerning this mystic presence in the world. It appears in several logia in the Coptic version and in a slightly different, and more understandable, form in the Greek version (Oxyrhynchus 1).

Logion 30.

Jesus said,
Where there are three gods, gods they are.
Where there are two or one, I am with him.

Logion 77.

Jesus said,
I am the Light which is above them all.
I am the All.
The All came forth from me.
The All attained to me.
Cut wood in two, I am there.
Pick up a stone, you will find me there (in it?).

Oxyrhynchus 1.

Jesus says,
Where there are two, they are not without God.
Where there is one, I say that I am with him.
Pick up a stone, there (in it?) you will find me.
Cut wood in two, I am also there.

At first glance, particularly in the Coptic Thomas version, this sounds a strong note of pantheism. In the Oxyrhynchus Greek version it is a most *comforting* pantheism to say that one does not get away from the presence of God in Christ.

Where two are together, God is there.
If only one is there, he is not without the presence of Christ.
The trees speak of his presence.
The rocks echo that voice.

That type of "pantheism" does not repel.

THE WORLD

Even in the mild Gnosticism reflected in the *Gospel of Thomas* the "world" is conceived of in a dualistic theme. There is this *world below* and there is the *world above*. The one is *material;* the other is *spiritual.* The one is man's *gaol;* the other is man's *goal.* But he can escape that *gaol* and reach that *goal* only if he finds the "gnosis."

This material world *according* to Logion 12 was created for "James, the righteous" and yet it is an evil world. In all of Gnostic writing the world is corrupt and in others (not in Thomas) it was created by a corrupt god.

This world is not worthy of one who has found the "gnosis" (Logion 56); one must be on guard against it (Logion 21). To understand the true nature of this world is to understand that it is a corpse (Logia 56, 60, 80). One must not depend upon it (Logion 87). It is to be stripped off as one would strip off old clothes (Logia 21, 37), an idea similar to Jesus' teaching in Matthew 6 (Logion 36) on the relative unimportance of clothes, very much like Paul's metaphorical teaching about putting off the old and putting on the new (Col. 3:8-14; Eph. 4:22-24).

It is the *world above* which is to be the goal of the one who has found the "gnosis." It is the world of "light" and "images" (Logia 83-84). The light is in the Father and it is concealed in his "image," his eternal nature. Those who have the "gnosis" also have "images" in that world above and seeing them will bring even greater rejoicing than receiving the "gnosis" and knowing one's true nature in this world. This is the earliest example discovered to date of the idea of major importance later in Manichaeism that these "Platonic" images in the world above are identified in some form of emanation with the elect below.

The true Gnostic is to seek this world above as an abiding treasure (Logion 76). It is the "place" where Jesus really dwells in "light" (Logion 24). It is the "place" of Life (Logion 4), a Life that is found through suffering (Logion 58).

MAN

In the *Gospel of Thomas* man, too, is a part of this dualistic theme. He is a creature of this world but his origin was in the world above and his goal is a return to that world. This appears to be the meaning of Logion 18.

> The disciples said to Jesus,
>   Tell us what our end will be like.
> Jesus said,
>   Have you already discovered the beginning
>   and now you ask about the end?
>   Where the beginning is, there
>   the end will be.
>   Blessed is the one who will
>   stand at the beginning
>   and will know the end
>   and will not taste death.

The "elect," the "solitary," have come from the kingdom of the Father and they will return to it (Logion 49). To know that one's origin is in that world above and that to leave this world below is to return to that world above is the blessed experience of the one who finds the "gnosis." Otherwise, to "taste death," which seems to mean to experience non-being, is his destiny.

Logion 19 continues this theme by pronouncing a blessing upon "him who was before he came to be." Such a one coming to be Jesus' disciple will find that even this material world has some service to render him, "the very stones will minister to you."

As a part of this material world, man is subject to death. Those who do not find the "gnosis," the enlightenment of God, have cause to be apprehensive of death (Logia 59, 70). For those who find the "gnosis," however, death holds no element of apprehension; to him the world itself is a corpse (Logion

56). His destiny is to be released from this world in its transitory nature and to be in perfect union with the Father (Logion 50) and all the other "solitaries" who, like himself, have found unity with the world of light (Logia 49, 61, 75).

SIN AND SALVATION

In the *Gospel of Thomas* sin and salvation are bound together as opposites. Sin is the negative of lacking salvation; salvation is the positive of being free from sin. Montefiore[13] observes that Gnosticism as reflected in Thomas is a religion of salvation but it is interpreted in a mystical and unbiblical way.

Sin is to hold on to material things and concerns. Salvation is to give up all such things. Thus, in Logion 36 the Gnostic is to have no concern from morning to night for such a mundane matter as clothing. To do so is sin; to refuse to do so is salvation. It was sin for the rich man in Logion 63 to think that he could nourish his *soul* with material goods. To deny food to the physical body is salvation (Logion 69); it is to find the kingdom (Logion 27).

To cling to material things as one clutches clothes about him is sin; to give up these things like children stripping off their clothes in innocent recognition that they do not need them is salvation (Logia 21, 37). To do this is to see the Son of the Living One and to be free of fear.

To cling to this-world ties, even within one's family, is sin; to hate father, mother, brothers, and sisters, and to follow Jesus in the way of the cross (death to this world) is salvation (Logion 55). This is repeated in Logion 101 with the additional emphasis that human mother-child relationship means birth unto death, but divine mother-child relationship means birth unto life.

To hold to formal "practices of religion" such as alms-giving, praying, and fasting, is sin (Logia 6, 14). One must even recognize that the most cherished expression of covenant relation-

---

[13]Montefiore, *op. cit.*, p. 91.

ship with God, circumcision, is unnecessary and of no value where the spiritual is concerned (Logion 53).

To experience salvation and freedom from sin, sex in its total impulse, expression, and even recognition, must be given up. To engage in sex is sin because it is to bring into the world more people who are born to the bondage of this world and of death (Logion 101). It is sin because it lacks the unity which comes in denying all recognition of differences and a resolving of all distinctions so there is no recognition of male and female. To attain such unity through the erasure of all differences is to enter the kingdom (Logion 22). Rather than have Mary Magdalene (whom Jesus had cleansed even to the casting out of "seven demons") banned from the group of his followers, Jesus said in Logion 114 that he would re-create her to be male like the other disciples in order that she might enter the kingdom of heaven.

THE KINGDOM AND ESCHATOLOGY

And what, in the *Gospel of Thomas,* is this "kingdom" into which men who have received the "gnosis" enter? It is at this point that Thomas is most like the Synoptics. While he prefers the term "kingdom of the Father" which is hardly known in the Synoptics, his views are closely parallel with the Synoptics in the idea of the "kingdom of heaven" or the "kingdom of God." This is evident when one views in parallel the "kingdom parables" in Thomas and in the Synoptics.

To read the twenty kingdom sayings in the *Gospel of Thomas* is to hear an echo of multiple words and ideas from the Synoptics. It is of this world; it is of the world above. It is present; it is invisible. It is inside you; it is outside you. It is realized; it is future. It should be observed, however, in the beginning, that in the *Gospel of Thomas,* where the kingdom is future the reference is to the "world above" rather than to the "world below." There is little place for some and no place for other ideas commonly associated with eschatological themes in the New Testament.

In the *Gospel of Thomas* death is present but it simply

means release from the evil material world for one who finds the "gnosis"; it appears to be the end of being for one who does not (Logion 11). There is no idea of man's resurrection in the *Gospel of Thomas*. There is no knowledge of the famous Oxyrhynchus fragment of a burial shroud bearing the words, "Jesus said, 'There is nothing buried which will not be raised up!'"

The Coptic version of Thomas even omits the one clear reference to resurrection contained in the Greek version. Oxyrhynchus 654 contains the words, "There is nothing buried which will not be raised up." Both Coptic Logia 5 and 6 omit this in the series. Death was freedom from the body. In line with their kindred-thinking Greek philosophers, the Gnostics had no place or desire for resurrection of the body.

There is no "judgment" in the eschatological sense in the *Gospel of Thomas*. To be *in the world* is to be under judgment. To be released from it is to be released from judgment. Grant[14] notes whimsically that, for the true Gnostic, *the world* is hell!

There is no clear reference in the *Gospel of Thomas* to the idea of a Second Coming of Christ. In Logion 12 the disciples speak of Christ's going away and of who will be their leader. They do not speak of his return, nor does he. In Logion 24 they ask Jesus to show them the place where he really dwells in order that they may seek it. They do not anticipate his "coming back," they anticipate going to dwell with him.

In Logion 37 they ask Jesus,

> When will you be revealed to us?
> When will we see you?

If they have a "Second Coming" in mind such as the *Parousia* of the New Testament, Jesus does not take it up. He answers, rather, that they will see him in his true nature when, like little children, they strip off the world and all its necessities. There is no Second Coming idea in that. There are no other possible references.

---

[14]R. M. Grant, *Gnosticism and Early Christianity* (New York: Columbia University Press, 1959), p. 150.

Eternal destiny is, for those who have the "gnosis," a return to the world of light, a return to the "kingdom" from which they have come (Logion 49). It is a destiny of freedom from the material. If there is in the *Gospel of Thomas* an "eternal destiny" for the unenlightened, those who do not find the "gnosis," it appears to be simply a matter of non-being beyond the death of the body.

Logion 11.

Jesus said,
>   This heaven will pass away, and the
>   one above it will pass away; and
>   the dead live not, and
>   the living die not.

It is clearly a "realized" kingdom, not a future one. It is immanent, not eminent.[15] The kingdom in the *Gospel of Thomas* is here and now. In Logion 51 the disciples asked Jesus when the state of "rest" for the dead would come and "when will the new world come?"

Jesus answered,
>   What you anticipate has come, but
>   you do not recognize it.

They were anticipating something which was present but not recognized.

In Logion 113 the disciples asked Jesus,

When will the kingdom come?

Jesus answered,
>   It will not come by anticipation.
>   They will not say, "Look, here" or
>   "Look, there."
>   Rather the kingdom of the Father
>   is spread out over the world
>   and men do not recognize it.

---

[15]Gaertner, *op. cit.*, pp. 211-17, has a helpful section on this aspect of the kingdom.

In Logion 3 the spiritual nature of the kingdom is under-
lined. Jesus said that the kingdom was *internal* and not *external*. He said that if it were external and in the skies, the birds
would have the advantage of it rather than men! And he said
if it were external and in the sea, the fish would have the advantage of it rather than men! But it is neither. He said,

> The kingdom is within you,
>   and it is without you,
> If you will come to know *yourselves*,
>   then you will be known by yourselves,
>   and you will understand that
>   you are sons of the Living Father.

In this world the kingdom exists only in men. To know one's
self as the son of the Living Father is to know that one is both
in the kingdom and *has the kingdom within* himself. The Naas-
sene Gnostics also emphasized that the kingdom was both inside and outside, both present and invisible.

What is this kingdom like? The disciples asked this in Logion
20. Jesus responded by telling the Parable of the Mustard Seed.
It is like what happens when an almost infinitesimally small
mustard seeds falls into *ploughed* (prepared) soil. There is in
it a principle of life which produces a tremendous plant, a plant
the size of which in its end is entirely out of proportion to its
beginning. This could be repeated by a review of all the kingdom parables. There is mystery in its power and in its growth.
It is the greatest treasure which man may possess. To fail to
find it is blindness. To fail to value it is tragedy.

How does one come to experience this kingdom? The answer
to that question is perhaps best realized in one of the *Gospel of
Thomas* sayings which is most like the Jesus of the Synoptics,
i.e., Logion 82.

> Jesus said,
>   The one who is near me is near the fire.
>   The one who is far from me is far
>   from the kingdom.

Identification with Jesus envelops one in the fire of God's presence which Jesus brings. To stand off in refusal to identify with Jesus is to be far from the kingdom, and to be far from the kingdom is to be without God, both for the world which is below and the world which is above.

THESE

ARE THE SECRET WORDS
WHICH THE LIVING JESUS SPOKE
AND DIDYMUS JUDAS THOMAS WROTE.
WHOEVER FINDS THE MEANING OF THESE WORDS,
WILL NOT TASTE DEATH!

THOMAS AND CANONICAL PARALLELS

(See also the following Index for Comparative Reference)

These are the secret words which the Living Jesus spoke and Didymus Judas Thomas wrote.

1. And he said,
He who discovers the interpretation of these words will not taste death!

2. Jesus said,
Let the seeking one not stop seeking until he finds.
When he finds he will be troubled and being troubled he will marvel.
Then he will reign over the All.

3. Jesus said,
If those trying to entice you say to you, "Look, the kingdom is in heaven," then the birds will have an advantage over you.
If they say to you, "Look, it is in the sea," then the fish will have an advantage over you.
But the kingdom is inside you and outside of you. When you really understand yourselves then you will be understood and you will know that *you* are the sons of the Living Father.
But if you do not understand yourselves, you will be in poverty and you will be poverty.

4. Jesus said,
The man who is old in days will not hesitate to ask an infant of seven days about the place of Life, and he will live.
For there are many who are first who will become last, and they will become a single one.

"But many *who are* first will be last; and *the* last, first."   19:30

5. Jesus said,
Know what is in your sight, and what is concealed will be revealed.
Because there is nothing concealed which will not be revealed.

6. His disciples asked him,
Do you wish us to fast? How should we

"And behold, *some* are last who will be first, and *some* are first who will be last."   13:30

"But many *who are* first, will be last; and the last, first." Mark 10:31

"For nothing is hidden that shall not become evident, nor *anything* secret that shall not be known and come to light."   8:17

"For nothing is hidden, except to be revealed; nor has *anything* been secret, but that it should come to light."
                          Mark 4:22

pray? How should we give alms?
What diet should we keep?
Jesus said,
Do not lie.
Do not what you hate. Because all
things are manifest in the sight of
heaven.
Because there is nothing concealed
which will not be revealed, and nothing covered up which will not be un-
covered.

". . . for there is nothing covered that
will not be revealed, and hidden that
will not be known."   10:26

7. Jesus said,
Blessed is the lion which a man eats and
the lion becomes a man.
Cursed is the man whom a lion eats and
the lion becomes man [or, and the
man becomes lion?].

8. And he said,
A man is like a wise fisherman who cast
his net into the sea. He drew it up
from the sea full of small fish. Among
them that wise fisherman found one
large good fish. He threw all the
small fish back into the sea and without one regret chose the big fish.

47. "Again, the kingdom of heaven is
like a drag-net cast into the sea, and
gathering *fish* of every kind;
48. and when it was filled, they drew
it up on the beach; and they sat down,
and gathered the good *fish* into con-
tainers, but the bad they threw away.
49. "So it will be at the end of the
age; the angels shall come forth, and
take out the wicked from among the
righteous,
50. and will cast them into the furnace
of fire; there shall be weeping and
gnashing of teeth."   13:47-50

Whoever has ears to hear let him
hear.

"He who has ears to hear, let him
hear."   11:15
(also 13:9,43)

9. Jesus said,
Look, a sower went out to sow. He filled
his hand and scattered. Some fell on
the path; the birds came and har-
vested them!

3. . . . "Behold, the sower went out to
sow;
4. and as he sowed, some *seeds* fell beside the road, and the birds came and
devoured them.

Others fell on the rock; they sent no
root down to the earth and no ear up
to heaven!

5. "And others fell upon rocky places,
where they did not have much soil; and
immediately they sprang up, because
they had no depth of soil.

6. "But when the sun had risen, they
were scorched; and because they had
no root, they withered away.

"But there is nothing covered up that
will not be revealed, and hidden that
will not be known."   12:2

Identical in Luke 8:8; 14:35.

Identical in Mark 4:9, 23; 7:16; Rev.
2:7, 13:9.

5. "The sower went out to sow his seed;
and as he sowed, some fell beside the
road; and it was trampled under foot,
and the birds of the air devoured it.

3. . . . "Behold, the sower went out to
sow;
4. and it came about that as he was
sowing, some *seed* fell beside the road,
and the birds came and ate it up.

6. "And other *seed* fell on rocky *soil,*
and as soon as it grew up, it withered
away, because it had no moisture.

5. "And other *seed* fell on the rocky
ground where it did not have much
soil; and immediately it sprang up because it had no depth of soil.

6. "And after the sun had risen, it was
scorched; and because it had no root,
it withered away.

Others fell among thorns; these choked the seed and the worms ate them.

Others fell on good soil; it produced good fruit, sixty to one, and one hundred twenty to one.

7. "And others fell among the thorns, and the thorns came up and choked them out.

8. "And others fell on the good soil, and yielded a crop, some a hundred fold, some sixty, and some thirty."
13:3-8

[See also 13:18-23 for allegorizing interpretation absent in the Thomas parable.]

10. Jesus said,
I have cast a fire upon the earth, and, behold, I watch over it until it blazes up.

11. Jesus said,
This heaven shall pass away and the one which is above it shall pass away. The dead shall not live; the living shall not die.
When you ate that which was dead you made it alive.
When you enter the light what will you do?
When you were one, you became two but when you become two what will you do?

"Heaven and earth will pass away, but My words shall not pass away."
24:35 (cf.5:18)

12. The disciples said to Jesus,
We know that you will depart from us. Who is the one who will be great [rule] over us?
Jesus said to them, wherever you go, go to James the Righteous for whose sake heaven and earth came to be.

13. Jesus said to his disciples,
Make a comparison to me and tell me whom I am like.
Simon Peter said to him, You are like a righteous angel.
Matthew said to him, You are like a wise man of understanding [a philosopher].
Thomas said to him,
My mouth [tongue] cannot say whom you are like.

13. Now when Jesus came into the district of Caesarea Philippi, He *began* asking His disciples, saying, "Who do people say that the Son of Man is?"

14. And they said, "Some *say* John the Baptist; some, Elijah; and others, Jeremiah, or one of the prophets."

15. He said to them, "But who do you say that I am?"

7. "And other *seed* fell among the thorns; and the thorns grew up with it, and choked it out.

8. "And other *seed* fell into the good ground, and grew up, and produced a crop a hundred times as great. . . ."
8:5-8

[See also 8:11-15 for Luke's version of allegorizing interpretation.]

7. "And other *seed* fell among the thorns, and the thorns grew up and choked it, and it yielded no crop.

8. "And other *seeds* fell into the good soil and as they grew up and increased, they were yielding a crop and were producing thirty, sixty, and a hundredfold."
Mark 4:3-8

[See also 4:14-20 for Mark's version of the allegorizing interpretation.]

"I have come to cast fire upon the earth; and how I wish it were already kindled!"
12:49

"Heaven and earth will pass away, but My words will not pass away."
21:33
(cf. 16:17)

"Heaven and earth will pass away, but My words will not pass away."
Mark 13:31

18. And it came about that while He was praying alone, the disciples were with Him, and He questioned them, saying, "Who do the multitudes say that I am?"
19. And they answered and said, "John the Baptist; but others *say,* Elijah; and others, that one of the prophets of old has risen again."

20. And He said to them, "But who do you say that I am?" And Peter an-

27. And Jesus went out, along with His disciples, to the villages of Caesarea Philippi; and on the way He questioned His disciples, saying to them, "Who do people say that I am?"
28. And they told Him, saying, "John the Baptist; and others *say* Elijah; but still others, one of the prophets."

29. And He *continued* by questioning them, "But who do you say that I

16. And Simon Peter answered and said,
"You are the Christ, the Son of the
living God."
17. And Jesus answered and said to
him, "Blessed are you, Simon Barjonas,
because flesh and blood did not reveal *this* to you, but My Father who is
in heaven."   16:13-20

Jesus said,
I am no longer your Master because you
    have become intoxicated, you have
    drunk from the bubbling spring which
    I have sent out.
Then he took him aside; he spoke
    three words to him.
When Thomas returned to his compan-
    ions, they asked him,
    What did Jesus say to you?

Thomas answered,
    If I speak one of the words which he
    said to me, you will take up stones
    and throw them at me. Then fire will
    come out of the stones and burn you
    up.

14. Jesus said to them,
If you fast, you will beget for yourself
    sin.
If you pray you will be damned.
If you give alms, you will do evil to
    your spirit.

If you go into any country and travel in
    its regions, if they receive you, eat
    what they set before you. Heal the
    sick among them. Because what goes
    into your mouth will not defile you,
    but what comes out of your mouth
    is what defiles you.

15. Jesus said,
When you see him who was not born of
    woman, fall upon your faces and wor-
    ship him; he is your Father.

16. Jesus said,
Men think perhaps that I have come
    to cast peace upon the world. They
    do not know that I have come to

See Matt. 6:1-18 for an opposite teaching on fasting, praying, and giving.

"Heal *the* sick, . . ."   10:8
"Not what enters into the mouth defiles the man, but what proceeds out of
the mouth, this defiles the man." 15:11

34. "Do not think that I came to bring
peace on the earth; I did not come to
bring peace, but a sword.

102

swered and said, "The Christ of God."

am?" Peter answered and said to Him, "You are the Christ."

21. But He warned them, and instructed *them* not to tell this to anyone, 9:18-21

30. And He warned them to tell no one about Him.   Mark 8:27-30

8. "And whatever city you enter, and they receive you, eat what is set before you;
9. and heal those in it who are sick, . . ."   10:8-9

If one of the unbelievers invites you . . . . eat anything that is set before you. . . .   1 Cor. 10:27
". . . There is nothing outside the man which going into him can defile him; but the things which proceed out of the man are what defile the man."
                              Mark 7:15

49. "I have come to cast fire upon the earth; and how I wish that it were already kindled!"

cast divisions upon the earth, fire, sword, war.

Because there will be five in a house: three will be against two and two against three; father against son and son against father. They will stand as solitaries.

35. "For I come to set a man against his father, and a daughter against her mother, and a daughter-in-law against her mother-in-law;
36. and a man's enemies will be the members of his household."   10:34-36

17. Jesus said,
I will give to you: What eye has not seen; What ear has not heard; What hand has not touched; What has not entered the heart of man.

18. The disciples said to Jesus,
Tell us what our end will be.
Jesus said,
Have you then discovered the beginning so that you ask about the end? Where the beginning is, there the end will be.
Blessed is the one who will stand at the beginning and will know the end and will not taste death.

19. Jesus said,
Blessed is the one who was before he came into being.
If you become my disciples and hear my words, these stones will serve you.
Because you have five trees in Paradise which are not changed in summer or winter; their leaves do not fall. He who understands them will not taste death.

20. The disciples said to Jesus,
Tell us what the kingdom of heaven is like. He said to them,
It is like a mustard seed, smaller than all seeds. But whenever it falls on ploughed soil, it puts forth a large branch and becomes a shelter for the birds of heaven.

31. He presented another parable to them, saying, "The kingdom of heaven is like a mustard seed, which a man took and sowed in his field;
32. and this is smaller than all *other* seeds; but when it is full grown, it is larger than the garden plants, and becomes a tree, so that the birds of the

104

51. "Do you suppose that I came to grant peace on earth? I tell you, no, but rather division;
52. for from now on five *members* in one household will be divided, three against two, and two against three.
53. "They will be divided, father against son, and son against father; mother against daughter, and daughter against mother; mother-in-law against daughter-in-law, and daughter-in-law against mother-in-law."   12:49, 51-53

. . . . but just as it is written,
"Things which eye has not seen and ear has not heard,

And *which* have not entered the heart of man . . ."   1 Cor. 2:9
[See also Isa. 64:4; 65:17]

18. Therefore He was saying, "What is the kingdom of God like, and to what shall I compare it?
19. "It is like a mustard seed, which a man took and threw into his own garden; and it grew and became a tree; and the birds of the air nested in its branches."   13:18-19

30. And He said, "How shall we picture the kingdom of God, or by what parable shall we present it?
31. "*It is* like a mustard seed, which when sown upon the ground, though it is smaller than all the seeds that are upon the ground,
32. yet when it is sown, grows up and

air come and nest in its branches."
13:31-32

21. Mary said to Jesus,
Whom are your disciples like?
He said,
They are like little children who have
taken their place in a field which does
not belong to them.
When the ones who own the field
come, they will say, Let us have our
field.
They [the children] will strip off their
clothes before them to release and
return to them their field.
Therefore I say, If the master of the
house knows the thief is coming, he
will stay awake until he comes and
not let him dig through into his kingdom house to carry off his goods.
You, therefore must watch for the
world; gird up your loins with power
lest the robbers find a way to come at
you, for they will find the advantage
for which you look.
Let there be among you one prudent
man; when the fruit was ripe, he
came quickly, sickle in hand, and
reaped it.
Whoever has ears to hear, let him hear.

43. "But be sure of this, that if the
head of the house had known at what
time of the night the thief was coming, he would have been on the alert
and would not have allowed his house
to be broken into.
44. "For this reason you be ready too;
for the Son of Man is coming at an
hour when you do not think *He will*."
24:43-44

22. Jesus saw little children who were
receiving their mother's milk. He said
to his disciples,
These children who are receiving milk
are like the ones who enter the king-
dom. They asked him,
Shall we, too, being children enter the
kingdom? Jesus said to them,
When you make the two one,
When you make the inside as the out-
side,
When you make the top as the bottom
When you make male and female into
a single, so the male is not male and
the female is not female,
When you make eyes an eye,
When you make the hand a hand,
When you make the foot a foot,

1. At that time the disciples came to
Jesus, saying, "Who then is greatest in
the kingdom of heaven?"
2. And He called a child to Himself
and stood him in their midst,
3. and said, "Truly I say to you, unless
you are converted, and become like
children, you shall not enter the kingdom of heaven."
18:1-3

becomes larger than all the garden plants and forms large branches; so that the birds of the air can nest under its shade."

                        Mark 4:30-32

39. "And be sure of this, that if the head of the house had known at what hour the thief was coming, he would not have allowed his house to be broken into.

40. "You too, be ready; for the Son of Man is coming at an hour that you do not expect."

                        12:39-40

47. But Jesus, knowing what they were thinking in their heart, took a child and stood him by His side,

48. and said to them, "Whoever receives this child in My name receives Me; and whoever receives Me receives Him who sent Me; for he who is least among you, this is the one who is great."

                        9:47-48

35. And sitting down, He called the twelve and said to them, "If anyone wants to be first, he shall be last of all, and servant of all."

36. And taking a child, He stood him in the midst of them; and taking him in His arms, He said to them,

37. "Whoever receives one child like this in My name is receiving Me; and whoever receives Me is not receiving Me, but Him who sent Me."

                        Mark 9:35-37

An image, an image—
Then you will enter!

23. Jesus said,
I have chosen you, one out of a thousand, two out of ten thousand; they
will stand as a single one.

24. His disciples said,
Show us the place where you are since
it is necessary for us to seek it.
He said to them,
Whoever has ears let him hear.
Inside a man of light, there is light and
he lights the entire world. When he
does not shine there is darkness.

25. Jesus said,
Love your brother as your own soul.
Guard him as the apple of your eye.

17. ". . . keep the commandments."
18. He said to Him, "Which ones?"
And Jesus said, "You shall not commit
murder; . . .;
19. . . . and you shall love your neighbor as yourself."   19:17-19
[See also 22:39]

26. Jesus said,
The speck which is in your brother's eye
you see, but the log which is in your
own eye, you do not see.

When you cast the log out of your own
eye, then you will see clearly to cast
the speck out of your brother's eye.

27. [Jesus said]
If you do not fast from the world, you
will not find the kingdom.
If you do not keep the Sabbath as Sabbath, you will not see the Father.

28. Jesus said,
I stood in the midst of the world; in
flesh I was manifest to them. I found
all of them drunk. I found not one
of them thirsting.
My soul suffered for the sons of men
because in their heart they are blind;
they do not see that they came into
the world empty; they seek to leave
the world again, empty.

3. "And why do you look at the speck
in your brother's eye, but do not notice
the log that is in your own eye?
4. "Or how can you say to your brother,
'Let me take the speck out of your eye,'
and behold, the log is in your own eye?
5. "You hypocrite, first take the log out
of your own eye; and then you will see
clearly *enough* to take the speck out of
your brother's eye."   7:3-5

LUKE	OTHER

... "You shall love the Lord your God with all your heart, . . .; and your neighbor as yourself."   10:27

". . ., 'You shall love your neighbor as yourself.' There is no other commandment greater . . ."   Mark 12:31

41. "And why do you look at the speck that is in your brother's eye, but do not notice the log that is in your own eye?
42. "Or how can you say to your brother, 'Brother, let me take out the speck that is in your eye,' when you yourself do not see the log that is in your own eye? You hypocrite, first take the log out of your own eye, and then you will see clearly to take out the speck that is in your brother's eye."
6:41-42

109

But now they are drunk; when they throw off their wine, then they will repent.

29. Jesus said,
If the flesh has come to be because of the spirit, it is a marvel.
If the spirit has come to be because of the body, it is a marvel of marvels.
But I marvel at how this treasure has made its home in poverty.

30. Jesus said,
Where there are three gods, gods they are.
Where there are two or one, I am with him.

"For where two or three have gathered together in My name, there I am in their midst." 18:20

31. Jesus said,
No prophet is acceptable in his village;

. . . "A prophet is not without honor except in his home town, and in his *own* household." 13:57

no physician heals those who know him.

32. Jesus said,
A city which is built on a high mountain, fortified, cannot fall nor be hidden.

"A city set on a hill [or mountain] cannot be hidden." 5:14

33. Jesus said,
What you hear in one ear and in the other, proclaim from your housetops.

". . . what you hear *whispered* in *your* ear, proclaim upon the housetops." 10:27

Because no one lights a lamp and puts it under a kitchen measure, nor in a hidden place.

"Nor do *men* light a lamp and put it under the peck-measure,

He puts it on a lampstand so all who come in and go out may see its light.

but on a lampstand; and it gives light to all who are in the house." 5:15

110

"... no prophet is welcome in his home town."   4:24

... "A prophet is not without honor except in his home town and among his *own* relatives and in his *own* household."   Mark 6:4
For Jesus Himself testified, that a prophet has no honor in his own country.   John 4:44

... "No doubt you will quote this proverb to Me, 'Physician, heal yourself; whatever we heard was done at Capernaum, do here in your home town as well.'"   4:23

"... what you have whispered in the inner rooms shall be proclaimed upon the housetops."   12:3

"Now no one after lighting a lamp covers it over with a container or puts it under a bed; but he puts it on a lampstand, in order that those who come in may see the light."   8:16
"No one, after lighting a lamp, puts it away in a cellar, nor under a peck-measure, but on the lampstand, in order

"A lamp is not brought to be put under a peck-measure, is it, or under a bed? Is it not *brought* to be put on the lampstand?"   Mark 4:21

THOMAS	MATTHEW

34. Jesus said,
If a blind man leads a blind man, both will fall into a pit.

".... And if a blind man guides a blind man, both will fall into a pit."
15:14

35. Jesus said,
It is impossible for one to go into a strong man's house and take it, unless by force he binds his hands. Then he will plunder the house.

"Or how can anyone enter the strong man's house and carry off his property, unless he first binds the strong *man?* And then he will plunder his house."
12:29

36. Jesus said,
From morning to night and from night to morning do not be distracted about what you will wear.

"For this reason I say to you, do not be anxious for your life, *as to* what you shall eat, or what you shall drink; nor for your body, *as to* what you shall put on. . . ."
6:25

"Do not be anxious then, saying, 'What shall we eat?' or 'What shall we drink?' or 'With what shall we clothe ourselves?' "
6:31

37. His disciples asked,
When will you be manifest to us? When will we see you?
Jesus said,
When you strip off your clothes without shame and take your clothes and trample them under your feet as little children, then [you will see?] the Son of the Living and you will not fear.

38. Jesus said,
Many times you have yearned to hear these words which I am speaking to you, and you have no other one from whom to hear them.
There will be days when you will seek me; you will not find me.

39. Jesus said,
The Pharisees and the scribes have received the keys of knowledge; they have hidden them. They did not enter nor did they let those who wished [enter].

"But woe to you, scribes and Pharisees, hypocrites, because you shut off the kingdom of heaven from men, for you do not enter in yourselves; nor do you allow those who are entering to go in."
23:13

that those who enter may see the light."
11:33

... "A blind man cannot guide a blind
man, can he? Will they not both fall
into a pit?" 6:39

"But no one can enter the strong man's
house and plunder his property unless
he first binds the strong man, and then
he will plunder his house." Mark 3:27

... "For this reason I say to you, do
not be anxious for *your* life, *as to* what
you shall eat; nor for your body, *as to*
what you shall put on. 12:22

"And do not seek what you shall eat,
and what you shall drink, and do not
keep worrying." 12:29

"Woe to you lawyers! For you have
taken away the key of knowledge; you
did not enter in yourselves, and those
who were entering in you hindered."
11:52

But you, be wise as serpents and innocent as doves.

"Behold, I send you out as sheep in the midst of wolves; therefore, be shrewd as serpents, and innocent as doves."
        10:16

40. Jesus said,
A vine has been planted apart from the Father; since it has not grown, it will be pulled up roots and all and destroyed.

But He answered and said, "Every plant which My heavenly Father did not plant shall be rooted up." 15:13

41. Jesus said,
To him who has in his hand shall be given and from him who does not have shall be taken even the little he does have.

"For whoever has, to him shall *more* be given, and he shall have an abundance; but whoever does not have, even what he has shall be taken away." 25:29

42. Jesus said,
Become passers-by.

43. His disciples asked him,
Who are you that you should say these things to us?
Jesus answered them,
From what I say to you, you do not recognize who I am?
You have become like the Jews:
They love the tree and hate the fruit;
They love the fruit and hate the tree!

44. Jesus said,
Whoever blasphemes against the Father, it shall be forgiven him.
But whoever blasphemes against the Holy Spirit, it shall not be forgiven —not on earth; not in heaven.

31. "Therefore I say to you, any sin and blasphemy shall be forgiven men; but blasphemy against the Spirit shall not be forgiven.
32. "And whoever shall speak a word against the Son of Man, it shall be forgiven him; but whoever shall speak against the Holy Spirit, it shall not be forgiven him, either in this age, or in the *age* to come." 12:31-32

45. Jesus said,
They do not gather grapes from thorns nor figs from thistles because they bear no fruit.

"You will know them by their fruits. Grapes are not gathered from thornbushes, nor figs from thistles, are they?"
        7:16

A good man brings forth what is good out of his treasure.

34. "You brood of vipers, how can you, being evil, speak what is good? For the

"Therefore take care how you listen; for whoever has, to him shall *more* be given; and whoever does not have, even what he thinks he has shall be taken away from him."   8:18

For whoever has, to him shall *more* be given; and whoever does not have, even what he has shall be taken away from him."   Mark 4:25

"And everyone who will speak a word against the Son of Man, it shall be forgiven him; but he who blasphemes against the Holy Spirit, it shall not be forgiven him."   12:10

28. "Truly I say to you, all sins shall be forgiven the sons of men, and whatever blasphemies they utter;
29. but whoever blasphemes against the Holy Spirit never has forgiveness, but is guilty of an eternal sin;"
                                Mark 3:28-29

44. "For each tree is known by its own fruit. For men do not gather figs from thorns, nor do they pick grapes from a briar bush.

45. "The good man out of the good treasure of his heart brings forth what

A bad man brings forth what is evil out of his evil treasure, his heart, and he speaks evil.

Because out of what fills his heart he brings forth evil.

mouth speaks out of that which fills the heart.

35. "The good man out of *his* good treasure brings forth what is good; and the evil man out of *his* evil treasure brings forth what is evil."   12:34-35

46. Jesus said,

From Adam to John the Baptist among those born of women there is no one greater than John the Baptist, in order that his eyes will not be broken.

But I say that he among you who becomes childlike shall know the kingdom and shall become greater than John.

"Truly, I say to you, among those born of women there has not arisen *anyone* greater than John the Baptist;

yet he who is least in the kingdom of heaven is greater than he."   11:11

47. Jesus said,

It is not possible for a man to ride two horses nor bend two bows.

And it is not possible for a slave to be a slave to two masters. Or [if he is] he will obey the one and [in so doing] offend the other.

"No one can serve two masters; for either he will hate the one and love the other, or he will hold to one and despise the other. You cannot serve God and Mammon."   6:24

No one drinks old wine and immediately desires to drink new wine.

They do not put new wine into old wineskins lest they burst.

And they do not pour old wine into new wineskins, lest it spoil them.

"Nor do *men* put new wine into old wine-skins; otherwise the wine-skins burst, and the wine pours out, and the wine-skins are ruined; but they put new wine into fresh wine-skins, and both are preserved."   9:17

They do not sew an old patch on a new garment because a tear would result.

"But no one puts a patch of unshrunk cloth on an old garment; for the patch pulls away from the garment, and a worse tear results."   9:16

48. Jesus said,

If two in a house make peace with one another, they shall say to the mountain, "Be moved," and it will be moved.

". . . for truly I say to you, if you have faith as a mustard seed, you shall say to this mountain, 'Move from here to there,' and it shall move; and nothing shall be impossible to you."   17:20

"Again I say to you, that if two of you agree on earth about anything that they may ask, it shall be done for them by My Father who is in heaven."   18:19

is good; and the evil *man* out of the evil *treasure* brings forth what is evil; for his mouth speaks from that which fills his heart."   6:44-45

"I say to you, among those born of women, there is no one greater than John;

yet he who is least in the kingdom of God is greater than he."   7:28

"No servant can serve two masters; for either he will hate the one, and love the other, or else he will hold to one and despise the other. You cannot serve God and Mammon."   16:13
"And no one, after drinking old *wine* wishes for new; for he says, 'The old is good *enough.*'"   5:39

"And no one puts new wine into old wine-skins; otherwise the new wine will burst the skins, and it will be spilled out, and the skins will be ruined." 5:37
"But new wine must be put into fresh wine-skins."   5:38

. . . "No one tears a piece from a new garment and puts it on an old garment; otherwise he will both tear the new, and the piece from the new will not match the old."   5:36

22. "And no one puts new wine into old wine-skins; otherwise the wine will burst the skins, and the wine is lost, and the skins *as well;* but *one puts* new wine into fresh wine-skins." Mark 2:22

"No one sews a patch of unshrunk cloth on an old garment; otherwise the patch pulls away from it, the new from the old, and a worse tear results."
      Mark 2:21

49. Jesus said,
Blessed are the solitary and elect; you
shall find the kingdom because you
have come from it and you shall go
there again.

50. Jesus said,
If they ask you, "What is your source?,"
answer them, "We have come from
the Light, the place where the Light
came to be of itself. It [came to be]
and it revealed itself in their image."
If they ask you, "Who are you?," answer, "We are his sons; we are the
chosen of the Living Father."
If they ask you, "What is the sign of
your Father's presence in you?," answer, "It is a movement and a rest."

51. His disciples asked him,
When will the rest (repose) of the
dead come to be; when will the new
world come?
He answered them,
What you anticipate has already come
but you do not recognize it.

52. His disciples said to him,
Twenty-four prophets spoke in Israel;
they all spoke of you.
He said to them,
You have ignored the Living One who
is in your presence and have spoken
about those who are dead.

53. His disciples asked him, Is circumcision profitable or not? He answered
them,
If it were profitable, their father would
beget them from their mother already
circumcised.
The real circumcision in spirit is alto-
gether profitable.

54. Jesus said,
Blessed are the poor, for yours is the
kingdom of heaven.

55. Jesus said,
He who does not hate his father and his
mother cannot be my disciple and
[he who does not] hate his brothers

"Blessed are the poor in spirit, for theirs
is the kingdom of heaven."   5:3

37. "He who loves father or mother
more than Me is not worthy of Me;
and he who loves son or daughter more
than Me is not worthy of Me.

118

. . . "Blessed *are* you *who are* poor, for yours is the kingdom of God." 6:20

26. "If anyone comes to Me, and does not hate his own father and mother and wife and children and brothers and sisters, yes, and even his own life, he can-

and sisters and take up his cross after me will not be worthy of me.

38. "And he who does not take his cross and follow after me is not worthy of Me."   10:37-38

56. Jesus said,
He who has recognized the world has discovered a corpse; the world is not worthy of him.

57. Jesus said,
The kingdom of the Father is like a man who possessed seed. At night his enemy came and sowed a weed among the good seed. The man did not allow them to pull up the weed. He said to them, "By chance in pulling up the weed you may pull up the wheat with it. On the harvest day the weeds will appear plainly; they will pull them up and burn them.

24. He presented another parable to them, saying, "The kingdom of heaven may be compared to a man who sowed good seed in his field.
25. "But while men were sleeping, his enemy came and sowed tares also among the wheat, and went away.
26. "But when the wheat sprang up and bore grain, then the tares became evident also.
27. "And the slaves of the landowner came and said to him, 'Sir, did you not sow good seed in your field? How then does it have tares?'
28. "And he said to them, 'An enemy has done this!' And the slaves said to him, 'Do you want us, then, to go and gather them up?'
29. "But he said, 'No; lest while you are gathering up the tares, you may root up the wheat with them.
30. " 'Allow both to grow together until the harvest; and in the time of the harvest I will say to the reapers, "First gather up the tares; and bind them in bundles to burn them up; but gather the wheat into my barn." ' "   13:24-30
36. Then He left the multitudes, and went into the house. And His disciples came to Him, saying, "Explain to us the parable of the tares of the field."
37. And He answered and said, "The one who sows the good seed is the Son of Man,
38. and the field is the world; and *as for* the good seed, these are the sons of the kingdom; and the tares are the sons of the evil *one*;

not be My disciple.

27. "Whoever does not carry his own cross and come after Me cannot be My disciple."   14:26-27

39. and the enemy who sowed them is the devil, and the harvest is the end of the age; and the reapers are angels.

40. "Therefore just as the tares are gathered up and burned with fire, so shall it be at the end of the age.

41. "The Son of Man will send forth His angels, and they will gather out of His kingdom all stumbling-blocks, and those who commit lawlessness,

42. and will cast them into the furnace of fire; in that place there shall be weeping and gnashing of teeth.

43. "Then the righteous will shine forth as the sun in the kingdom of their Father. He who has ears, let him hear."
13:36-43

58. Jesus said,
Blessed is the man who has suffered, he has discovered the life.

59. Jesus said,
Look upon the Living One as long as you live, lest you die and seek to see him and not be able to.

60. (——) a Samaritan carrying a lamb on his way to Judea. He said to his disciples.
"[Why is] the man [carrying] the lamb with him?"
They answered,
"That he may kill it and eat it."
He said to them,
"While it remains alive, he will not eat it, but only when he kills it and it becomes a corpse."
They answered,
"Otherwise he will not be able to do [eat] it.
He said to them,
"You, seek a place of rest for yourselves lest you become a corpse and be consumed."

61. Jesus said,
Two will lie down to rest on a bed.
The one will die; the other will live.

Salome said,
Who are you, O man? Whose [son]?
You who have reclined on my couch
and eaten from my table? Jesus answered her,
I am he who is from the One who is
the same [with me]. To me has been
given the things of My Father.
[Salome said]
I am your disciple.
[Jesus said]
Therefore I say, whenever one is one
he will be filled with light, but whenever he is divided, he will be filled
with darkness.

62. Jesus said,
I speak my mysteries to the ones
[worthy of?] my mysteries.

Whatever your right (hand) does, do   "But when you give alms, do not let
not let your left (hand) know what   your left hand know what your right
it does.   hand is doing;"   6:3

63. Jesus said,
There was a rich man who had many
useful things. He said, I will use my
useful things in order that I may
sow and reap and plant and fill my
barns with fruit, that I may lack
nothing.
Such were the thoughts in his heart and
he died that night.
Whoever has ears let him hear.

64. Jesus said,
A man had guests. When he prepared a   2. "The kingdom of heaven may be
dinner, he sent his servant in order   compared to a king, who gave a wed-
that he might invite the guests.   ding feast for his son.

124

16. And He told them a parable, saying, "The land of a certain rich man was very productive.

17. "And he began reasoning to himself, saying, 'What shall I do, since I have no place to store my crops?'

18. "And he said, 'This is what I will do: I will tear down my barns and build larger ones, and there I will store all my grain and my goods.

19. 'And I will say to my soul, "Soul, you have many goods laid up for many years *to come*; take your ease, eat, drink *and* be merry." '

20. "But God said to him, 'You fool! This *very* night your soul is required of you; and *now* who will own what you have prepared?'

21. "So is the man who lays up treasure for himself, and is not rich toward God."　　　　　　　　　12:16-21

(See also parallels to Logion 8)

16. But He said to him, "A certain man was giving a big dinner, and he invited many;

He went to the first and said to him, "My master invites you." He said, "I have investments with some merchants; they are coming to me this very night; I will meet them and give them orders. I beg to be excused from the dinner."

He went to another and said to him, "My master has invited you." He said to him, "I have purchased a house and they request a day [of settlement] of me. I will not have time."

He went to another and said to him, "My master invites you." He said to him, "My friend is to be married and I am preparing a dinner; I cannot come. I beg to be excused from the dinner."

He went to another and said to him, "My master invites you." He said to him, "I have bought a field; I am going to collect the rent. I beg to be excused."

The servant returned and said to his master, "The ones whom you invited to the dinner have begged to be excused."

The master said to the servant, "Go out to the streets and bring the ones you find in order that they may dine. Traders and merchants shall not come into my Father's places."

3. "And he sent out his slaves to call those who had been invited to the wedding feast, and they were unwilling to come.

4. "Again he sent out other slaves saying, 'Tell those who have been invited, "Behold, I have prepared my dinner; my oxen and my fattened livestock are *all* butchered and everything is ready; come to the wedding feast." '

5. "But they paid no attention and went their way, one to his own farm, another to his business,

6. and the rest seized his slaves and mistreated them and killed them.

7. "But the king was enraged and sent his armies, and destroyed those murderers, and set their city on fire.

8. "Then he said to his slaves, 'The wedding is ready, but those who were invited were not worthy.

9. 'Go therefore to the main highways, and as many as you find *there*, invite to the wedding feast.'

10. "And those slaves went out into the streets, and gathered together all they found, both evil and good; and the wedding hall was filled with dinnerguests.

11. "But when the king came in to look over the dinner-guests, he saw there a man not dressed in wedding clothes;

12. and he said to him, 'Friend, how did you come in here without wedding clothes?' And he was speechless.

17. and at the dinner hour he sent his slave to say to those who had been invited, 'Come; for everything is ready now.'
18. "But they all alike began to make excuses. The first one said to him, 'I have bought a piece of land and I need to go out and look at it; please consider me excused.'
19. "And another one said, 'I have bought five yoke of oxen, and I am going to try them out; please consider me excused.'
20. "And another one said 'I have married a wife, and for that reason I cannot come.'

21. "And the slave came *back* and reported this to his master. Then the head of the household became angry and said to his slave, 'Go out at once into the streets and lanes of the city and bring in here the poor and crippled and blind and lame.'
22. "And the slave said, 'Master, what you commanded has been done, and still there is room.'
23. "And the master said to the slave, 'Go out into the highways and along the hedges, and compel *them* to come in, that my house may be filled.
24. 'For I tell you, none of those men who were invited shall taste of my dinner.'"   14:16-24

127

13. "Then the king said to the servants, 'Bind him hand and foot, and cast him into the outer darkness; in that place there shall be weeping and gnashing of teeth.'

14. "For many are called, but few *are* chosen."   22:2-14

65. He said,

A good (kind) man owned a vineyard. He leased it to husbandmen in order that they might work it and in order that he might receive from them its fruit.

He sent servants that the husbandmen might give him the fruit of the vineyard. They seized the servant, beat him and almost killed him. The servant returned and reported it to his master.

His master said, "Perhaps he did not recognize them" [probably should be, "perhaps they did not recognize him"]. He sent another servant; the husbandmen beat him too.

Then the owner sent his son saying, "Perhaps they will have respect for my son."

Since the husbandmen recognized that this was the heir of the vineyard they seized and killed him.

Whoever has ears let him hear.

33. "Listen to another parable. There was a landowner who planted a vineyard and put a wall around it and dug a winepress in it, and built a tower, and rented it out to vine-growers, and went on a journey.

34. "And when the harvest time approached, he sent his slaves to the vine-growers to receive his produce.

35. "And the vine-growers took his slaves and beat one, and killed another, and stoned a third.

36. "Again he sent another group of slaves larger than the first; and they did the same thing to them.

37. "But afterward he sent his son to them, saying, 'They will respect my son.'

38. "But when the vine-growers saw the son, they said among themselves, 'This is the heir; come, let us kill him, and seize his inheritance.'

39. "And they took him, and cast him out of the vineyard, and killed *him.*

40. "Therefore when the owner of the vineyard comes, what will he do to those vine-growers?"

41. They said to Him, "He will bring those wretches to a wretched end, and will rent out the vineyard to other vine-growers, who will pay him the proceeds at the *proper* seasons."   21:33-41

66. Jesus said,

Show me the stone which the builders rejected; it is the corner stone.

Jesus said to them, "Did you never read in the Scriptures, 'The stone which the builders rejected, This became the chief corner-stone . . .'?"   21:42

67. Jesus said,

He who knows the All but has failed [to know] himself lacks all.

128

9. And He began to tell the people this parable: "A man planted a vineyard and rented it out to vine-growers, and went on a journey for a long time.
10. "And at the *harvest* time he sent a slave to the vine-growers, in order that they might give him *some* of the produce of the vineyard; but the vine-growers beat him and sent him away empty-handed.
11. "And he proceeded to send another slave; and they beat him also and treated him shamefully, and sent him away empty-handed.
12. "And he proceeded to send a third; and this one also they wounded and cast out.
13. "And the owner of the vineyard said, 'What shall I do? I will send my beloved son; perhaps they will respect him.'
14. "But when the vine-growers saw him, they reasoned with one another, saying, 'This is the heir; let us kill him that the inheritance may be ours.'
15. "And they cast him out of the vineyard and killed him. What, therefore, will the owner of the vineyard do to them?
16. "He will come and destroy those vine-growers and will give the vineyard to others." And when they heard it, they said, "May it never be!"   20:9-16

And He began to speak to them in parables: "A man planted a vineyard, and put a wall around it, and dug a vat under the winepress, and built a tower, and rented it out to vine-growers and went on a journey.
2. "And at the *harvest* time he sent a slave to the vine-growers, in order to receive *some* of the produce of the vineyard from the vine-growers.
3. "And they took him, and beat him, and sent him away empty-handed.
4. "And again he sent them another slave, and they wounded him in the head, and treated him shamefully.
5. "And he sent another, and that one they killed; and *so with* many others, beating some, and killing others.
6. "He had one more *to send*, a beloved son; he sent him last *of all* to them, saying, 'They will respect my son.'
7. "But those vine-growers said to one another, 'This is the heir; come, let us kill him, and the inheritance will be ours!'
8. "And they took him, and killed him, and threw him out of the vineyard.
9. "What will the owner of the vineyard do? He will come and destroy the vine-growers, and will give the vineyard to others."   Mark 12:1-9

But He looked at them and said, "What then is this that is written, '*The* stone which the builders rejected, This became the chief cornerstone'?"   20:17

"Have you not even read this scripture: 'The stone which the builders rejected, This became the chief corner-stone . . .'?"   Mark 12:10

68. Jesus said,

Blessed are you whenever you are persecuted but no place will be found
[for them?] where you have been persecuted.

69. Jesus said,

Blessed are the ones who have been
persecuted in their heart; these are
the ones who have known the Father
in truth.

Blessed are the hungry, because the
belly of the one who hungers will be
filled.

70. Jesus said,

Whenever you bring out [to share?]
that which you have within you, that
which you have [and share?] will save
you.
If you do not have [for sharing?] that
which is within you, that which you
do not have [for sharing?] within
you will destroy you.

71. Jesus said,

I will [destroy?] this house and no one
will be able to build it.

72. (———) to him, "Command my
brothers in order that they may divide
my father's possessions with me."

He said to him,

"O man, who made me a divider?"

He turned to his disciples and said to
them,

"I am not a divider, am I?"

73. Jesus said,

On the one hand the harvest is great,
on the other hand the workers are
few; pray the Lord in order that he
may send workers into the harvest.

74. He said,

Lord, there are many standing about
the spring, but no one is in the spring.

75. Jesus said,

Many are standing near the door, but
the solitaries are the ones who will
go into the bridal chamber.

"Blessed are you when *men* revile you,
and persecute you, and say all kinds of
evil against you falsely, on account of
Me."   5:11

"Blessed are you when *men* revile you,
and persecute you, and say all kinds of
evil against you falsely, on account of
Me."   5:11

"Blessed are those who hunger and
thirst for righteousness, for they shall
be satisfied."   5:6

"Blessed are you when men hate you,
and ostracize you, and heap insults
upon you, and spurn your name as evil,
for the sake of the Son of Man." 6:22

13. And someone in the crowd said to
Him, "Teacher, tell my brothers to divide the *family* inheritance with me."
14. But He said to him, "Man, who ap-
pointed Me a judge or arbiter over
you?"   12:13-14

And He was saying to them, "The
harvest is plentiful, but the laborers are
few; therefore beseech the Lord of the
harvest to send laborers into His harvest."   10:2

76. Jesus said,
The kingdom of the Father is like a
man who was a merchant [travelling]
with his merchandise [pack]; he discovered a pearl.
That merchant was wise. He sold the
merchandise, he purchased the one
pearl for himself.
You, too, seek the treasure which does
not fail, which endures where no
moth approaches to devour and no
worm to destroy.

45. "Again, the kingdom of heaven is
like a merchant seeking fine pearls,
46. and upon finding one pearl of great
value, he went and sold all that he had,
and bought it." 13:45-46

19. "Do not lay up for yourselves treasures upon earth, where moth and rust
destroy, and where thieves break in and
steal;
20. but lay up for yourselves treasures
in heaven, where neither moth nor rust
destroys, and where thieves do not
break in or steal;" 6:19-20

77. Jesus said,
I am the light which is above All;
I am All;
The All originated in Me, and
The All has come unto me.
Split wood in two; I am there [in it?].
Pick up a stone, there [in it?] you will
find me.

78. Jesus said,
Why did you go into the desert? To see
a reed bent by the wind? To see a
man clothed in soft clothes?
(———)kings and high standing ones
are the ones who are clothed in soft
clothes and they are not able to know
the truth.
[Note: Jesus seems to be speaking of
himself.]

7 . . . "What did you go out into the
wilderness to look at? A reed shaken
by the wind?
8. "But what did you go out to see?
A man dressed in soft *clothing?* Behold, those who wear soft *clothing* are
in kings' palaces." 11:7-8
[Note: Jesus is speaking of John the
Baptist.]

79. A woman in the crowd said to him,
Blessed is the womb which bore you
and the breasts which fed you. He
said to her,
Blessed are the ones who have heard
the Father's word and kept it in truth
because there will be days when you
will say, "Blessed is the womb which
has *not* borne and the breasts which
have *not* given milk.

"But woe to those who are with child
and to those who nurse babes in those
days!" 24:19

"Sell your possessions and give to charity; make yourselves purses which do not wear out, an unfailing treasure in heaven, where no thief comes near, nor moth destroys."   12:33

24. . . . He began to speak to the multitudes about John, "What did you go out into the wilderness to look at? A reed shaken by the wind?
25. "But what did you go out to see? A man dressed in soft clothing? Behold, those who are splendidly clothed and live in luxury are *found* in royal palaces.   7:24-25

27. And it came about while He said these things, one of the women in the crowd raised her voice, and said to Him, "Blessed is the womb that bore You and the breasts at which You nursed."
28. But He said, "On the contrary, blessed are those who hear the word of God, and observe it."   11:27-28

"Woe to those who are with child and to those who nurse babes in those days; for there will be great distress upon the

"But woe to those who are with child and to those who nurse babes in those days!"   Mark 13:17

80. Jesus said,
The one who has recognized the world
   has discovered the body [corpse?]
   and whoever has discovered the body
   [corpse?], of him the world is not
   worthy.

81. Jesus said,
Let the one who has become rich be
   king, and let the one who has power
   renounce it.

82. Jesus said,
He who is near me is near the fire and
   he who is far from me is far from the
   kingdom.

83. Jesus said,
The images are revealed to man and
   the light in them is concealed in the
   image of the light of the Father.
He will reveal himself and his image
   is hidden by his light.

84. Jesus said,
When you see your likeness you rejoice.
   But when you see your images which
   came to be before you, which do not
   die nor are revealed, how much [of
   such sight?] will you be able to bear?

85. Jesus said,
Adam came to be out of great power
   and richness, but he did not come to
   be worthy of you.
If he had been worthy, he would not
   have died.

86. Jesus said,
[The foxes] have their dens and the
   birds have their roosting places but
   the Son of Man has no place to lay
   his head and rest.

. . . "The foxes have holes, and the
birds of the air *have* nests; but the Son
of Man has nowhere to lay His head."
8:20

87. Jesus said,
Wretched is the body which depends on

land, and wrath to this people, . . ."
21:23

"For behold, the days are coming when they will say, 'Blessed are the barren, and the wombs that never bore, and the breasts that never nursed.' " 23:29

. . . "You are not far from the kingdom of God." . . .   Mark 12:34

. . . "The foxes have holes, and the birds of the air *have* nests, but the Son of Man has nowhere to lay His head."
9:58

a body, and
Wretched is the soul which depends
upon the two [body and soul].

88. Jesus said,
The angels and the prophets will come
to you and give you what is yours.
You, also will give them what is in your
hands and say to yourselves, "On
what day will they come and take
what belongs to them?"

89. Jesus said,
Why do you wash the outside of the
cup?

"You blind Pharisee, first clean the inside of the cup and of the dish, so that
the outside of it may become clean
also."   23:26

Do you not realize that the one who
made the inside is also the one who
made the outside?

90. Jesus said,
Come to me,

28. "Come to Me, all who are weary
and heavy laden, and I will give you
rest.
29. "Take My yoke upon you, and learn
from Me, for I am gentle and humble
in heart; and you shall find rest for
your souls.

because my yoke is easy, my lordship gentle, and you shall find for
yourselves, rest.

30. "For My yoke is easy, and My load
is light."   11:28-30

91. They said to him,
Tell us who you are in order that we
may believe in you.

He said to them,
You check the appearance of the sky
and the earth,

2. But He answered and said to them,
"When it is evening, you say, 'It will
be fair weather, for the sky is red.'
3. "And in the morning, 'There will be
a storm today, for the sky is red and
threatening.'

and the one who is in your presence
you do not recognize?
You do not know how to test this time.

Do you know how to discern the appearance of the sky, but cannot discern
the signs of the times?"   16:2-3

39. But the Lord said to him, "Now you Pharisees clean the outside of the cup and of the platter; but inside of you, you are full of robbery and wickedness.
40. "You foolish ones, did not He who made the outside make the inside also?"

11:39-40

They said therefore to Him, "What then do You do for a sign, that we may see, and believe You? What work do You perform?"   John 6:30

"You hypocrites! You know how to analyze the appearance of the earth and the sky, but why do you not analyze this present time?"   12:56

92. Jesus said,
Seek and you will find.
Those things which you inquired of me
in those days I did not tell you.
Now I wish to tell them, but you do
not inquire of them.

93. Do not give that which is holy to
the dogs, lest they throw it on the
garbage pile.
Do not pour out pearls before swine, lest
they make it (——).

94. Jesus said,
The one who seeks will find (——)
it will be opened to him.

95. [Jesus said?],
If you have money do not invest it for
interest; rather give it to the one from
whom you will get nothing in return.

96. Jesus said,
The kingdom of the Father is like a
woman who took leaven [and put it]
in dough and made large loaves of it.
Whoever has ears let him hear.

97. Jesus said,
The kingdom of the [Father?] is like
a woman carrying a jar full of meal.
While she was walking on a long road,
the handle of the jar broke. The meal
spilled out behind her on the road.
She did not know. She had noticed no
trouble.
When she entered her house, she put
the jar down. She found it empty.

98. Jesus said,
The kingdom of the Father is like a
man who wants to kill a strong man.
He drew his sword while in his house,
and thrust it into the wall in order
to know if his hand would push it
through.
Then he killed the strong man.

". . . seek, and you shall find; . . ." 7:7

"Do not give what is holy to dogs,
and do not throw your pearls before
swine, lest they trample them under
their feet, and turn and tear you to
pieces."   7:6

". . . and he who seeks finds; and to
him who knocks it shall be opened."
                                    7:8

He spoke another parable to them;
"The kingdom of heaven is like leaven,
which a woman took, and hid in three
pecks of meal, until it was all leavened."   13:33

" . . . and he who seeks finds; and to him who knocks it shall be opened."
11:10

20. And again He said, "To what shall I compare the kingdom of God?
21. "It is like leaven, which a woman took and hid in three pecks of meal, until it was all leavened."   13:20-21

99. The disciples said to him,
Your brothers and your mother are
standing outside. He said to them,

47. And someone said to Him, "Behold,
Your mother and Your brothers are
standing outside seeking to speak to
You."
48. But He answered the one who was
telling Him and said, "Who is My
mother and who are My brothers?"
49. And stretching out His hand toward
His disciples, He said, "Behold, My
mother and My brothers!

Those in here who are doing the will
of my Father are my brothers and my
mother.
These are the ones who will enter the
kingdom of my Father.

50. "For whoever shall do the will of
My Father who is in heaven, he is My
brother and sister and mother."
12:47-50

100. They showed Jesus a gold coin
and said to him,
Caesar's men request taxes from us.
He said to them,

16. And they sent their disciples to
Him, along with the Herodians, saying,
"Teacher, we know that You are truthful and teach the way of God in truth,
and defer to no one; for You are not
partial to any.
17. "Tell us therefore, what do You
think? Is it lawful to give a polltax to
Caesar, or not?"

18. But Jesus perceived their malice,
and said, "Why are you testing Me,
you hypocrites?
19. "Show Me the coin *used* for the
poll-tax." And they brought Him a
denarius.
20. And He said to them, "Whose likeness and inscription is this?"
21. They said to Him, "Caesar's." Then
He said to them, "Then render to Caesar the things that are Caesar's; and to
God the things that are God's."
22:16-21

Give to Caesar Caesar's things.
Give to God God's things.
Give to me my things.

101. [Jesus said?]
The one who does not hate his father
and his mother in my way will not
be able to be my disciple.

"He who loves father or mother more
than Me is not worthy of Me; and he
who loves son or daughter more than
Me is not worthy of Me." 10:37

And the one who does [not] love [his
father] and his mother in my way
will not be able to be my disciple.
Because my mother [gave me death?]
but [my] true [mother] gave me life.

140

20. And it was reported to Him, "Your mother and Your brothers are standing outside, wishing to see You."

32. And a multitude was sitting around Him, and they said to Him, "Behold, Your mother and Your brothers are outside looking for You."

33. And answering them, He said, "Who are My mother and My brothers?"

34. And looking about on those who were sitting around Him, He said, "Behold, My mother and My brothers!

21. But He answered and said to them, "My mother and My brothers are these who hear the word of God and do it."
8:20-21

35. "For whoever does the will of God, he is My brother and sister and mother."
Mark 3:32-35

21. And they questioned Him, saying, "Teacher, we know that You speak and teach correctly, and You are not partial to any, but teach the way of God in truth.

13. And they sent some of the Pharisees and Herodians to Him, in order to trap Him in a statement.
14. And they came and said to Him, "Teacher, we know that You are truthful, and defer to no one; for You are not partial to any, but teach the way of God in truth. Is it lawful to pay a poll-tax to Caesar, or not?

22. "Is it lawful for us to pay taxes to Caesar, or not?"

15. "Shall we pay, or shall we not pay?" But He, knowing their hypocrisy, said to them, "Why are you testing Me? Bring Me a denarius to look at."
16. And they brought one.

23. But He detected their trickery and said to them,
24. "Show Me a denarius.

Whose head and inscription does it have?" And they said, "Caesar's."
24. And He said to them, "Then render to Caesar the things that are Caesar's, and to God the things that are God's."
20:21-25
"If anyone comes to Me, and does not hate his own father and mother and wife and children and brothers and sisters, yes, and even his own life, he cannot be My disciple."
14:26

And He said to them, "Whose likeness and inscription is this?" And they said to Him, "Caesar's."
17. And Jesus said to them, "Render to Caesar the things that are Caesar's, and to God the things that are God's." And they were amazed at Him.
Mark 12:13-17

141

102. Jesus said,

Woe to the Pharisees because they are like a dog sleeping in the manger of oxen.

He neither eats nor does he let the oxen eat!

103. Jesus said,

Blessed is the man who knows when the robbers will come, in order that he may arise and take up his [clothes? or arms?] and gird up his loins before they enter.

"But be sure of this, that if the head of the house had known at what time of the night the thief was coming, he would have been on the alert and would not have allowed his house to be broken into."   24:43

104. They said,

Come, let us pray and fast today.

Jesus said,

What is the sin I have committed or in what have I been overcome?

Rather, whenever the bridegroom comes from the bridal chamber, then let them fast and pray.

14. Then the disciples of John came to Him, saying, "Why do we and the Pharisees fast, but your disciples do not fast?"

15. And Jesus said to them, "The attendants of the bridegroom cannot mourn, as long as the bridegroom is with them, can they? But the days will come when the bridegroom is taken away from them, and then they will fast."   9:14-15

105. Jesus said,

The one who knows his father and mother, shall he be called son of a harlot?

106. Jesus said,

Whenever you make the two to be one you will become sons of man and when you say, "Mountain, move," it will move.

107. Jesus said,

10. "See that you do not despise one of these little ones, for I say to you, that their angels in heaven continually behold the face of My Father who is in heaven.

11. ["For the Son of Man has come to save that which was lost.]

"And be sure of this, that if the head of the house had known at what hour the thief was coming, he would not have allowed his house to be broken into."   12:39

33. And they said to Him, "The disciples of John often fast and offer prayers; the *disciples* of the Pharisees also do the same; but Yours eat and drink."
34. And Jesus said to them, "You cannot make the attendants of the bridegroom fast while the bridegroom is with them, can you?
35. "But *the* days will come; and when the bridegroom is taken away from them, then they will fast in those days."
                                    5:33-35

18. And John's disciples and the Pharisees were fasting; and they came and said to Him, "Why do John's disciples and the disciples of the Pharisees fast, but Your disciples do not fast?"
19. And Jesus said to them, "While the bridegroom is with them, the attendants of the bridegroom do not fast, do they? So long as they have the bridegroom with them, they cannot fast.
20. "But the days will come when the bridegroom is taken away from them, and then they will fast in that day."
                              Mark 2:18-20

Now all the tax-gatherers and the sinners were coming near Him to listen to Him.
2. And both the Pharisees and the scribes *began* to grumble, saying, "This man receives sinners and eats with them."

143

The kingdom is like a shepherd who had a hundred sheep.

One of them strayed away, the largest one. He left the ninety-nine and searched for the one until he found it.

Having wearied himself he said to the sheep, I love you beyond [more than] the ninety-nine.

12. "What do you think? If any man has a hundred sheep, and one of them has gone astray, does he not leave the ninety-nine on the mountains and go and search for the one that is straying? 13. "And if it turns out that he finds it, truly I say to you, he rejoices over it more than over the ninety-nine which have not gone astray."   18:10-13

108. Jesus said,

The one who drinks from my mouth will become as I am and I will become as he is and the secret things will be revealed to him.

109. Jesus said,

The kingdom is like a man who had a treasure in his field without knowing it.

And he died; he left it to his son. The son did not know; he received the field and then sold it.

He who purchased it went out and while plowing found the treasure.

He began to lend money to anyone he wished.

"The kingdom of heaven is like a treasure hidden in the field; which a man found and hid; and from joy over it he goes and sells all that he has, and buys that field."   13:44

110. Jesus said,

The one who has discovered the world has become rich; let him deny the world.

111. Jesus said,

The heavens will be curled up before your face and the one who lives in the Living One will see neither death nor fear, because Jesus says, "The

3. And He told them this parable, saying,

4. "What man among you, if he has a hundred sheep and has lost one of them, does not leave the ninety-nine in the open pasture, and go after the one which is lost, until he finds it?

5. "And when he has found it, he lays it on his shoulders, rejoicing.

6. "And when he comes home, he calls together his friends and his neighbors, saying to them, 'Rejoice with me, for I have found my sheep which was lost!'

7. "I tell you that in the same way, there will be *more* joy in heaven over one sinner who repents, than over ninety-nine righteous persons who need no repentance."   15:1-7

one who discovers himself, of him the world is not worthy."

112. Jesus said,
Woe to the flesh which depends on the soul;
Woe to the soul which depends on the flesh.

113. His disciples said to him,
When will the kingdom come?
[He said],
It will not come by anticipation. They will not say, "Look, here," or "Look, there."
Rather, the kingdom of the Father is spread out over the earth and men do not see it.

114. Simon Peter said to them,
Let Mary depart from us because women are not worthy of the Life.
Jesus said,
Look, I will lead her so that I will change her to male, in order that she also may become a living spirit like you males.
For every female who makes herself male will enter the kingdom of heaven.

**The Gospel According
to Thomas**

20. Now having been questioned by the Pharisees as to when the kingdom of God was coming, He answered them and said, "The kingdom of God is not coming with signs to be observed; 21. nor will they say, 'Look, here *it is!*' or 'There it is!' For behold, the kingdom of God is in your midst." 17:20-21

INDEX FOR COMPARATIVE REFERENCE

Thomas Saying	Canonical Parallel	Canonical Similarity
Prologue		John 11:16; 20:24
1		John 8:51-52
2		Matt. 7:7-8; Luke 11:9-10
3		Luke 17:21
4	Matt. 19:30; Mark 10:31; Luke 13:30	Matt. 11:25; Luke 10:21
5	Mark 4:22; Luke 8:17	
6	Matt. 10:26; Luke 12:2	Matt. 6:1-18; 7:12; Luke 6:31; Eph. 4:25; Col. 3:9
7	None	None
8	Matt. 13:47-50 Matt. 11:15 (also in Matt. 13:9,43; Mark 4:9,23; 7:16; Luke 8:8; 14:35; Rev. 2:7; 13:9)	
9	Matt. 13:3-9; Mark 4:3-9; Luke 8:5-8	
10	Luke 12:49	
11	Matt. 5:18; Luke 16:17 Matt. 24:35; Mark 13:31; Luke 21:33	1 Cor. 7:31; 1 John 2:17
12		Matt. 18:1; Mark 9:34; Luke 9:46
13	Matt. 16:13-16; Mark 8:27-30; Luke 9:18-21	
14	Luke 10:8; 1 Cor. 10:27 Matt. 10:8; Luke 10:9 Matt. 15:11; Mark 7:15	
15	None	None
16	Matt. 10:34; Luke 12:49 Matt. 10:35-36; Luke 12:51-53	
17	1 Cor. 2:9	
18	None	None
19		John 8:51-52; Rev. 2:7; 22:2
20	Matt. 13:31-32; Mark 4:30-32; Luke 13:18-19	
21	Matt. 24:43-44; Luke 12:39-40	Many short phrases
22	Matt. 18:1-3; Mark 9:35-37;	Matt. 19:13-15; Mark 10:13-

148

Thomas Saying	*Canonical Parallel*	*Canonical Similarity*
	Luke 9:47-48	15; Luke 18:15-17
		Gal. 3:28
23		Matt. 22:14; John 6:70; 13:18; 15:16,19
24		John 14:4-5 and many other short phrases
25	Matt. 19:17-19; 22:39; Mark 12:31; Luke 10:27	
26	Matt. 7:3-5; Luke 6:41-42	
27	None for certain	None for certain
28		1 Tim. 3:16
29	None	None
30	Matt. 18:20	
31	Matt. 13:57; Mark 6:4; Luke 4:23-24; John 4:44	
32	Matt. 5:14	Matt. 7:24-25
33	Matt. 10:27; Luke 12:3 Matt. 5:15; Mark 4:21; Luke 8:16; 11:33	
34	Matt. 15:14; Luke 6:39	
35	Matt. 12:29; Mark 3:27	Luke 11:21-22
36	Matt. 6:25,31; Luke 12:22,29	
37	None for certain	None for certain
38		Matt. 13:17; Luke 10:24 and other short phrases
39	Matt. 23:13; Luke 11:52 Matt. 10:16	
40	Matt. 15:13	John 15:1ff
41	Matt. 13:12; Mark 4:25; Luke 8:18	Matt. 25:29; Luke 19:26
42	None	None
43		John 14:8-11; Matt. 12:33; Luke 6:43-44 Matt. 7:17-20
44	Matt. 12:31-32; Mark 3:28-29; Luke 12:10	
45	Matt. 7:16; Luke 6:44-45 Matt. 12:34,35	
46	Matt. 11:11; Luke 7:28	

Thomas Saying	Canonical Parallel	Canonical Similarity
47	Matt. 6:24; Luke 16:13 Matt. 9:16-17; Mark 2:21-22; Luke 5:36-38	
48	Matt. 17:20; 18:19	Mark 11:23; 1 Cor. 13:2
49	None	None
50	None for certain	None for certain
51	None for certain	None for certain
52		Luke 24:5; John 5:39
53		Rom. 2:29; 1 Cor. 7:18-19; Gal. 6:15; Col. 2:11; Philip 3:3
54	Matt. 5:3; Luke 6:20	
55	Matt. 10:37-38; Luke 14:26-27	Matt. 16:24; Mark 8:34; Luke 9:23
56		Heb. 11:38
57	Matt. 13:24-30 (36-43)	
58		James 1:12; 1 Peter 3:14
59	None	None
60	None	None
61		Luke 17:34 and many short phrases
62	Matt. 6:3	Mark 4:11
63	Luke 12:16-21. See also parallels to Logion 8	
64	Matt. 22:2-14; Luke 14:16-24	
65	Matt. 21:33-41; Mark 12:1-9; Luke 20:9-16. See also parallels to Logion 8	
66	Matt. 21:42; Mark 12:10; Luke 20:17	1 Peter 2:4-6
67	None for certain	None for certain
68	Matt. 5:11; Luke 6:22	
69	Matt. 5:6, 11	
70	None	None
71		John 2:19
72	Luke 12:13-14	
73	Matt. 8:37-38; Luke 10:2	John 4:35
74	None	None
75		Matt. 22:10-14; 25:10

INDEX FOR COMPARATIVE REFERENCE

Thomas Saying	*Canonical Parallel*	*Canonical Similarity*
105		John 8:41
106	None	None
107	Matt. 18:10-13; Luke 15:1-7	
108		John 7:37
109	Matt. 13:44	
110	None	None
111		Several short phrases
112	None	None
113	Luke 17:20-21	
114	None	None

INDEX OF LOGIA

INDEX OF LOGIA

INDEX OF SCRIPTURES

INDEX OF SCRIPTURES

BIBLIOGRAPHY

Books

Bewick, Thomas (illustrator). *Aesop's Fables, a new translation for modern readers.* Mount Vernon: Peter Pauper Press, 1941.

Crum, W. E. *A Coptic Dictionary.* Oxford: At the Clarendon Press, 1939.

Dodd, C. H. *The Parables of the Kingdom.* New York: Charles Scribner's Sons, Ltd., 1956.

Doresse, Jean. *The Secret Books of the Egyptian Gnostics.* New York: The Viking Press, 1960.

Fowler, H. W. and F. G. (trans.). *The Works of Lucian of Samosata.* Vols. 1 and 3. Oxford: The Clarendon Press, 1949.

Gaertner, Bertil. *The Theology of the Gospel According to Thomas.* New York: Harper and Brothers, 1961.

Goodspeed, Edgar J. *A History of Early Christian Literature.* Revised by R. M. Grant. Chicago: The University of Chicago Press, 1966.

Grant, F. C. *The Gospels: Their Origin and Growth.* New York: Harper and Brothers, 1957.

Grant, R. M. *Gnosticism and Early Christianity.* New York: Columbia University Press, 1959.

_____ and Freedman, D. N. *The Secret Sayings of Jesus.* Garden City, N. Y.: Doubleday and Co., Inc., 1960.

_____ "Gnosticism," *The Interpreter's Dictionary of the Bible.* Vol. IV. New York: Abingdon Press, 1962.

Grobel, Kendrick. *The Gospel of Truth.* New York: Abingdon Press, 1960.

Grushkin, P. *Fables of Aesop.* New York: Archway Press, 1946.

Guillaumont, A.; Puesch, H. C.; Quispel, G.; Till, W.; and Y. A. A. Masih. *The Gospel According to Thomas.* New York: Harper and Brothers, 1959.

Hennecke, Edgar. *New Testament Apocrypha.* Edited by Wilhelm Schneemelcher. Vol. I. Philadelphia: The Westminster Press, 1963.

Jacobs, J. *The Fables of Aesop.* New York: The Macmillan Co., 1959.

Jeremias, Joachim. *The Parables of Jesus.* New York: Charles Scribner's Sons, Ltd., 1955.

_____. *Unknown Sayings of Jesus.* London: S.P.C.K., 1959.

Jonas, Hans. *The Gnostic Religion.* Boston: Beacon Press, 1958.

Labib, Pahor. *Coptic Gnostic Papyri in the Coptic Museum at Old Cairo.* Photographic plates, Vol. 1. Cairo: Government Press, 1956.

McKendry, J. J. *Aesop: Five Centuries of Illustrated Fables.* Greenwich, Conn.: The Metropolitan Museum of Art, 1964.

Metzger, Bruce M. *Lists of Words Occurring Frequently in the Coptic New Testament.* Grand Rapids: W. B. Eerdmans Publ. Co., 1961.

BIBLIOGRAPHY

Montefiore, Hugh, and Turner, H. E. W. *Thomas and the Evangelists.* Naperville, Ill.: Alec R. Allenson, Inc., 1962.

Murray, Margaret Alice. *Elementary Coptic (Sahidic) Grammar.* 2nd ed. London: Bernard Quaritch, 1927.

New American Standard Bible: New Testament. Nashville: Broadman Press, 1963.

Patri, A. *Aesop's Fables.* Philadelphia: J. B. Lippincott Co., 1949.

Plumley, J. Martin. *An Introductory Coptic Grammar.* London: Home and van Thal, 1948.

Robertson, A. T. *The Christ of the Logia.* Nashville: Sunday School Board of the S. B. C., 1924.

Streeter, B. H. *The Four Gospels.* London: Macmillan and Co., Ltd., 1924.

Taylor, Vincent. *The Gospels: A Short Introduction.* London: The Epworth Press, 1938.

van Unnik, W. C. *Newly Discovered Gnostic Writings.* Naperville, Ill.: Alec R. Allenson, Inc., 1960.

Wilson, R. M. *The Gnostic Problem.* London: A. R. Mowbray and Co., Ltd., 1964.

_____. *The Gospel of Philip.* New York: Harper & Row, Publishers, 1962.

_____. *Studies in the Gospel of Thomas.* London: A. R. Mowbray and Co., Ltd., 1960.

Articles

Betz, Hans Dieter. "The Logion of the Easy Yoke and the Rest," *Journal of Biblical Literature,* LXXXVI, Part I (March, 1967).

Quispel, Gilles. "Gnosticism," *Religions in Antiquity Seminar* (Hanover, N. H.: Dartmouth College Comparative Studies Center, 1966).

_____. "'The Gospel of Thomas' and 'The Gospel of the Hebrews,'" *New Testament Studies,* Vol. 12, No. 4 (July, 1966).

_____. "The Gospel of Thomas and the New Testament," *Vigilae Christianae,* XI, (1957).

_____. "Some Remarks on the Gospel of Thomas," *New Testament Studies,* Vol. 5, No. 4 (July, 1959).

Till, W. C. "New Sayings of Jesus in the Recently Discovered Coptic 'Gospel of Thomas,'" *Bulletin of the John Rylands Library,* XLI, 1959.

Wilson, R. M. "The Coptic 'Gospel of Thomas,'" *New Testament Studies,* Vol. 5, No. 4 (July, 1959).

BIBLIOGRAPHY

Unpublished Material

(Microfilm)

Akagi, Tai. "The Literary Development of the Gospel of Thomas" (unpublished Ph.D. dissertation, Western Reserve University, 1965).

Kim, Yong Ok. "The Christological Problem in the Gospel According to Thomas" (unpublished Ph.D. dissertation, Drew University, 1964).